Carrier of Christ's

"Arise, shine, for your light has come"

By Sheka Mansaray

DEDICATION

This book is dedicated to my Mother & Father who were not able to see these Light. May your souls rest in Peace.

Acknowledgements

I would like to gratefully and sincerely thank our Lord and savior Jesus Christ for all that He has done in my life, all the praise belongs to Him for keeping me focus for this book to be birth. I'm grateful and thankful for the grace to be able to be used by Him to bring others their Light and His truth.

This book is dedicated to my Mother & Father who were not able to see these Light. I would like to thank my wife, my strength, My best friend and My sweetness Nanah Mansaray, for her support, encouragement, quiet patience and unwavering love were undeniably the bedrock upon which the past four years of my life have been built. Happy 4th year Anniversary I'm forever blessed to spend more years with you and celebrate with you.

Finally, and most importantly, I thank God for my children Faith & Jeremiah and the family of Faith Embassy International Ministries for stand with me and pushing in prayer and support of the Vison, God will surely bless you all.

So, it is said: "Wake up, O sleeper, rise up from the dead, and Christ will shine on you."

Ephesians 5:1

Table constants

<u>1 Column</u>

Table constants

<u>2 Column</u>

Table constants

3 Column

Introduction

Hello everyone, welcome to a new life starting NOW …(you should know by now You are Designed for His Light, His Purpose & your Destiny) …You picked up this book or a friend told you about it and how great it is right? … By the opening of this wonderful book I believe that you will never forget and that you will always keep by your side. I do believe also that the vision and information shared in this book you will also share with friends and family.

This book "Carrier of Christ's Light" is one of many books coming. This book was five years in the making and now you are a light who get to read it and I'm sure you have heard those words before: "You are the salt of the earth. You are the light of the world." This is the year the Lord told me to put it out for many to partake of the anointing and Power of Light. This year of light, bring out the bright futures of God children. More over this year will pushing you/me to step into change to receive new blessings from the father. It is a year of new sites to step in too, new work to beginning, new connections with people and entering in to saving lives and wining souls for Jesus.

We are to always be in prayer to know and recognizing the times and seasons we are in is acknowledging the prophetic power of the season and what that means for your life. When you actively align yourself with what God is doing in this time, you will see breakthrough! As an Apostle, there will be apostolic and prophetic declarations of blessing over you to stir your faith and activate transformation in your life.

This book it is written for all those who are trying to find Christ our Lord and be steadfast to give us understanding on who is Jesus and how we can be the LIGHT that He brings to the world. This book is for you to connect onto our Lord and savior in prayer to show you the steps to take for your life. Also, as you read these books and the decrees within, say them out loud and continue declaring them over yourself for the days and weeks to come. Words are extremely powerful! Proverbs 18:21 says:

"The tongue has the power of life and death."

You have the choice to either bless or curse yourself with your words. Choose to bless yourself and be expectant for transformation to come.

Sometimes we hear something so often that we just assume that we know exactly what it means. But, we may have heard it so often that we have stopped thinking about what it means, and so it may have become just words, with no real meaning for our lives. And so, I don't think it hurts to occasionally look at some old familiar words and see if we can give them meaning again.

"You are the salt of the earth. You are the light of the world." Words first spoken by Jesus to his disciples. What did those words mean to them, and what might they still mean to us today? What if we had never heard the words, and someone came up to us and said, "You are the salt of the earth?" We might not be sure just what to think. Today, salt is a pretty common thing. It doesn't cost much. For some, it is even considered a bad thing, something the doctor says we should cut down on. We buy salt-free soup and salt-free crackers in order to be healthy. So being the "salt of the earth" may not sound like much of a compliment to us.

But it was different for the disciples. When Jesus first spoke those words, salt was a highly prized thing. Salt had many meanings and uses. It was a sign of loyalty and covenant fidelity, and was used in sacrifices made to God. Leviticus 2:13 reads; "you shall not omit from your grain offerings the salt of the covenant with your God; with all your offerings, you shall offer salt." Eating together was referred to as "Sharing Salt", and expressed a binding relationship.

Salt was used to purify, to season, and to preserve. Salt was precious.

And so for the disciples, Jesus was saying something significant. He was saying "you are valuable", "you are important, you make a difference in the world". And he was probably saying some other things as well. Salt was considered pure. In the same way, the disciples were to be pure. Jesus had just finished saying, "Blessed are the pure in heart." The disciples were to have an inner purity that reflected their devotion to God. They were to be examples of purity for others.

Salt also adds flavor. Maybe Jesus was also saying that a disciple's life should be an example of a rich and zestful life. A life of joy during the everyday consistency or blandness. Evidence that in serving God and following Christ there is excitement, and joy. Jesus probably meant all this and more in his simple statement, "You are the salt of the earth." To the disciples the statement was a compliment, and it was a challenge. Jesus also followed it with a warning. He said; ".... but if salt has lost its taste, how can its saltiness be restored? It is no longer good for anything, but is thrown out and trampled underfoot."

Jesus words serve as a warning that if the disciples deny their mission to be "salt of the earth', that they will be useless. Salt loses its saltiness by becoming impure, by becoming so mixed with other elements that it is no longer effective. To be effective, to stay "salty", the disciples had to stay focused on their mission, to know what they were to be about, to be pure,

to stay devoted to God. If they let their message be sort of "watered down" by the world, they would no longer have the power to be the "salt of the earth".

It may sound like most of the "salt-like" qualities are inner qualities. A sense of value, purity of heart, an attitude of zest and joy in life. But salt does not exist for itself, it is not of much value if kept to itself. In the same way, the disciples are not to exist for themselves. They are to live lives turned outward to the world. Jesus did not say, "You are salt", nonetheless, "You are the salt of the earth." It is taking those qualities of salt and giving them to the world that will make a difference.

If there is any doubt that Jesus expects the disciples to make a difference in the world, just look at what he says next; "You are the light of the world." The purpose of light is to shine, to enable people to see. The disciples are to be a light, to live as illumination for the world. Their faith is not to be purely personal and private. That would be like lighting a lamp and then hiding it under a bushel basket. Instead, they are to let their light shine, like putting it on a lampstand so that "it gives light to all in the house."

Jesus said, "Let you light shine before others, so that they may see your good works." The disciples were to be obvious about their faith. People were supposed to be able to see what they believed. Theirs was not to be a secret or private faith, but a faith that showed. but Jesus was clear about what the result of having their faith noticed was to be. He did not say, "Let you light shine before others, so that they may see your good works. And praise you", or, "Let you light shine before others, so that they may see your good works. And notice what a wonderful person you are and be impressed." He said, "Let you light shine before others, so that they may see your good works. And give glory to your Father in heaven."

Just as Jesus' deeds pointed not to his own glory but to the glory of God, so the purpose of the disciples' engaging in acts of faithfulness and righteousness was not for their own sakes, but to glorify God. The light the disciples had to give was generated by God. They had been given that light not for their own sakes, but for the sake of the world. They were to let that God-given light shine through their actions so that people would recognize God in them, and give God the glory. Jesus gave the disciples quite a bit to think about when he said, "You are the salt of the earth", and "You are the light of the world". And if we believe that we, too, are called to be his disciples, then all that he said applies to us, too. We are to be the "salt of the earth". Valuable, precious, pure, giving flavor. We are to be the "light of the world". Enabling others to see, pointing the way to Christ, giving glory to God.

Sometimes that is difficult to do. Sometimes we don't feel much like salt. Sometimes it is difficult for us to think of ourselves as precious, as valuable. But we have been created by God himself, and think of this poetically, have the understand and clarity that, God doesn't

make junk or junkie's! We are, as creations of God, precious and valuable. Sometimes it is difficult to be pure, to not let our faith get diluted or dulled by the world. And sometimes it is even difficult to feel a joy and zest for life, let alone spread that to others. Worries and just plain old day to day routines can rob us of the joy in Christ we should have. Sometimes we are just too discouraged, or too busy to feel much like being "the salt of the earth".

And sometimes we might not feel much like the "light of the world." Sometimes our light seems pretty dim, like it wouldn't be of much value to anyone. Sometimes we just plain get tired of trying to show everyone the way. People don't seem to pay too much attention or notice too much what we do, and sometimes it is tempting to say, "I've had enough of this shining business, let

someone else show the way!" Sometimes we'd like to just put our light under a bushel basket and forget it.

I think Jesus probably knew, even as he was saying those words, that they were not always going to be easy to believe or follow. Even though Jesus was fully divine, he was at the same time, fully human. A concept I think is hard for us to get ahold of. In his humanness, Jesus knew about the weaknesses and discouragements we live with day to day. But it is interesting that he did not say, "You are to try to be the salt of the earth, try to be the light of the world". Instead he said "You are the salt of the earth. You are the light of the world." He was not telling us to try to be something we are not, he was telling us to "Be what you are."

Jesus is not challenging us to try harder to be salt and light, but is telling us that as his followers, we are salt and light for the world. Jesus is not calling us to exert ourselves more in trying to become something we are not, but to believe Jesus' word and accept and live out what we are by his word and by the power of God. We are salt; precious, valuable, and pure; by the grace of God. We are lights, having been lit for the sake of the world, with the light of God. Welcome to a new life starting NOW.

1 Column

I have given you authority to trample on snakes and scorpions and to overcome all the power of the enemy; nothing will harm you Luke 10:19

As no one has power over the wind to contain it, so no one has power over the time of their death. As no one is discharged in time of war, so wickedness will not release those who practice it. Ecclesiastes 8:8

His divine power has given us everything we need for a godly life through our knowledge of him who called us by his own glory and goodness. 2 Peter 1:3

The source

The Son of God is the source of our longstanding, Jesus' identity is the assumption drawn from years of traditional thinking that the title "Son of God" must mean in the Scriptures an uncreated being, the member of an eternal Godhead. That notion cannot possibly be traced to the Scriptures. It is a testimony to the power of theological indoctrination that this idea persists so stubbornly.

In the Bible "Son of God" is an alternative and virtually synonymous title for the Messiah. Thus John dedicates his whole gospel to one dominant theme, that we believe and understand "that Jesus is the Messiah, the Son of God" (John 20:31). The basis for equating these titles is found in a favorite Old Testament passage in Psalm 2: "The rulers take counsel together against the LORD and against His Messiah" whom He has installed as King in Jerusalem (v. 6), and of whom He says: "Thou art My Son, today I have begotten thee. Ask of Me and I will give you the nations as your inheritance" (vv. 7, 8). Jesus does not hesitate to apply the whole Psalm to himself, and sees in it a prediction of his and his followers' future rulership over the nations (Rev. 2:26, 27).6 Peter makes the same equation of Messiah and Son of God, when by divine revelation he affirms his belief in Jesus: "Thou art the Messiah, the Son of the living God" (Matt. 16:16). The high priest asks Jesus: "Are you the Messiah, the Son of the blessed One?" (Mark 14:61).

Nathaniel understands that the Son of God is none other than the King of Israel (John 1:49), the Messiah (v. 41), "him of whom Moses in the Law and the Prophets wrote" (v. 45; cp. Deut. 18:15-18). The title "Son of God" is applied also in Scripture to angels (Job 1:6; 2:1; 38:7; Gen. 6:2, 4; Ps. 29:1; 89:6; Dan. 3:25), to Adam (Luke 3:38), to the nation of Israel (Exod. 4:22), to kings of Israel as representing God, and in the New Testament to Christians (John 1:12). We would search in vain to find any application of this title to an uncreated being, a member of the eternal Godhead. This idea is simply absent from the biblical idea of divine Sonship. Luke knows very well that Jesus' divine Sonship is derived from his conception in the womb of a virgin; he knows nothing at all any eternal origin: "The Holy Spirit will come upon you and the power of the Highest will overshadow you; for that reason, the holy thing which is begotten will be called the Son of God" (Luke 1:35). The Psalmist had ascribed the Messiah's Sonship to a definite moment of time—

"today" (Ps. 2:7). The Messiah was begotten around 3 BC (Matt. 1:20; Luke 1:35). His begetting is thus related to his appearance in history (Acts 13:33, not KJV), when God became his Father (Heb. 1:5; 1 John 5:18, not KJV). Here, clearly presented by the Scriptures which Jesus recognized as God's Word, are the biblical ideas of Jesus' Sonship. It is to be dated from Jesus' conception, "with power" from his

resurrection. He is God's Son at the same time as he is David's son (Rom. 1:3, 4). Luke's view of Sonship agrees exactly with the hope for the birth of the Messiah from the woman, a descendant of Adam, Abraham, and David (Matt. 1:1; Luke 3:38). The texts we have examined contain no information about a personal preexistence for the Son in eternity.

The Son of Man, the Lord at God's Right Hand The title "Son of Man" was frequently used by Jesus to refer to himself. Like "Son of God" it is closely associated with Messiahship; so much so that when Jesus solemnly affirms that he is the Messiah, the Son of God, he adds in the same breath that the high priest will see "the Son of Man sitting at the right hand of power and coming with the clouds of heaven" (Mark 14:61, 62). The title "Son of Man" is most fully described in Daniel 7:13, 14, where a human figure (a "Son of Man") receives the right to world dominion from the Father. The parallel with Psalm 2 is obvious, as well as the close connection with Psalm 110, where David refers to his "lord" (the Messiah) who is to sit at the Lord's (the Father's) right hand until he takes up his office as world governor and "rules in the midst of his enemies" (Ps. 110:2; cp. Matt. 22:42-45). The Son of Man has an equally clear Messianic connection in Psalm 80:17: "Let your hand be

upon your right-hand man, upon the Son of Man whom you made strong for yourself." It is significant that the New Testament writers lay the greatest stress on Psalm 110, citing it some 23 times

and applying it to Jesus, who had been by that time exalted as Messianic Lord to immortality at the right hand of the Father just as the Psalmist had foreseen. Once again we must recognize that eternal Sonship is alien to all the descriptive titles of the Messiah. This startling fact should lead Bible students everywhere to compare what they have been taught about Jesus with the Jesus presented by Scripture. It would appear that an eternal Son will not match the Bible's account of the Messiah. In opting for a Jesus who is an eternal being passing through a temporary life on earth, many seem, so to speak, to have "got the wrong man."

The Messiah

Jesus Claimed NOT to Be God In the Gospel of John the identity of Jesus is a principal theme. John wrote, as he tells us, with one primary purpose: to convince his readers that Jesus is "the Messiah, the Son of God" (20:31). According to John, Jesus carefully distinguished himself from the Father who is "the only true God" (17:3; cp. 5:44; 6:27). If we are to find in John's record a proof that Jesus is "coequal" God, in the Trinitarian sense, we would be discovering something which John did not intend and, in view of his Jewish heritage, would not have understood! Alternatively, we would have to admit that John introduces a brand new picture of Messiahship which contradicts the Old Testament and overthrows John's (and Jesus') own insistence that only the Father is truly God (John 5:44; 17:3). Such a glaring self-contradiction is hardly probable.7 It is high time that we allow Jesus to set the record straight. In Matthew's, Mark's, and Luke's accounts we are told that Jesus explicitly subscribed to the strict monotheism of the Old Testament (Mark 12:28-34). Did he therefore, according to John, confuse the issue by claiming after all to be God? The answer is given plainly in John 10:34-36 where Jesus defined his status in terms of the human representatives of God in the Old Testament. Jesus gave this account of himself in explanation of what it means to be "one with the Father" (10:30). It is a oneness of function by which the Son perfectly represents the Father. That is exactly the Old Testament ideal of sonship, which had been imperfectly realized in the rulers of Israel, but would find perfect fulfillment in the Messiah, God's chosen King.

The argument in John 10:29-38 is as follows: Jesus began by claiming that he and the Father were "one." It was a oneness of fellowship and function which on another occasion he desired also for his disciples' relationship with him and the Father (John 17:11, 22). The Jews understood him to be claiming

equality with God. This gave Jesus an opportunity to explain himself. What he was actually claiming, so he says, was to be "Son of God" (v. 36), a recognized synonym for Messiah. The claim to sonship was not unreasonable, Jesus argued, in view of the well-known fact that even imperfect representatives of God had been addressed by Him in the Old Testament as "gods" (Ps. 82:6). Far from establishing any claim to eternal Sonship, he compared his office and function to that of the judges. He considered himself God's representative par excellence since he was uniquely God's Son, the one and only Messiah, supernaturally conceived, and the object of all Old Testament prophecy. There is absolutely nothing, however, in Jesus' account of himself which interferes with Old Testament monotheism or requires a rewriting of the sacred text in Deuteronomy 6:4. Jesus' self-understanding is strictly within the limits laid down by God's authoritative revelation in Scripture. Otherwise his claim to be the Messiah would have been invalid. The Scriptures would have been broken.

John's Jewish Language Since Jesus expressly denied that he was God in John 10:3436, it will be most unwise to think that he contradicted himself elsewhere. John's Gospel should be examined with certain axiomatic principles firmly in mind. Jesus is distinct from "the only true God" (John 17:3). The Father alone is God (5:44). John wishes his readers to understand that all that he writes contributes to the one great truth that Jesus is the Messiah, the Son of God (20:31). Jesus himself says, as we have seen, that the term "god" can be used of a human being representing God, but certainly does not imply "coequal Godship." Jesus' own self-designation is plainly "Son of God" (John 10:36). In John 10:24, 25 Jesus told them "plainly" that he was the Messiah, but they did not believe him. Jesus states often that he has been "sent by God." What the average reader hears in that phrase is not at all what John implies.

John the Baptist was also "sent from God," which does not mean that he preexisted his birth (John 1:6). Prophets in general are "sent" from God (Judges 6:8; Micah 6:4), and the disciples themselves are to be "sent" as Jesus was "sent" (John 17:18). "Coming down from heaven" need not mean descent from a previous life any more than Jesus' "flesh, which is the bread which came down from heaven," literally descended from the sky (John 6:50, 51). Nicodemus recognized that Jesus had "come from God" (John 3:2), but did not think of him as preexistent. Nor did the Jewish people, when they spoke of the prophet "who was to come into the world" (John 6:14; cp. Deut 18:15-18), mean that he was alive before his birth. James can say that "every good thing bestowed and every perfect gift is from above, coming down from the Father" (James 1:17).

"Coming down from heaven" is Jesus' and the Jews' graphic way of describing divine origin, which certainly belonged to Jesus through the virgin birth. The "preexistence" statements in John (John 3:138; 6:62) are connected with the Son of Man, which means human being. The most that could be proved from these verses is that Jesus was a human being alive in heaven before he was born on earth! This sort of explanation is unnecessary, however, once it is noted that Daniel had 600 years earlier seen the Son of Man in vision seated at the right hand of the Father, a position which the New Testament says Jesus gained by resurrection and ascension. As Messiah, Jesus saw himself in the role of the one who was later to be exalted to heaven, since this, according to Daniel's inspired vision, was the destiny of the Messiah prior to his second coming in glory. Jesus does indeed "preexist" his future return to the earth. All this had been seen in advance by Daniel before the birth of the Messiah. Thus Jesus expected to ascend to the right hand of the Father where he had been seen before in vision as an exalted human being—Son of Man (John 6:62). To say that Jesus was actually at the Father's throne in heaven as a human being before his birth in Bethlehem is to misunderstand both John and Daniel. Jesus had to be born before anything predicted of him in the Old Testament could take place.

His own History

Glory Before Abraham Jesus found his own history written in the Hebrew Scriptures (Luke 24:27). The role of the Messiah was clearly outlined there. Nothing in the divine record had suggested that Old Testament monotheism would be radically disturbed by the appearance of the Messiah. A mass of evidence will support the proposition that the apostles never for one moment questioned the absolute oneness of God, or that the appearance of Jesus created any theoretical problem about monotheism. It is therefore destructive of the unity of the Bible to suggest that in one or two texts in John, Jesus overturned his own creedal statement that the Father was "the only true God" (17:3), or that he took himself far outside the category of human being by speaking of a conscious existence from eternity. Certainly his prayer for the glory which he had had before the world began (17:5) can be easily understood as the desire for the glory which had been prepared for him in the Father's plan.

The glory which Jesus intended for the disciples had also been "given" (John 17:22, 24), but they had not yet received it.9 It was typical of Jewish thinking that anything of supreme importance in God's purpose—Moses, the Law, repentance, the Kingdom of God and the Messiah—had "existed" with God from eternity. In this vein John can speak of the crucifixion having "happened" before the foundation of the world (Rev. 13:8, KJV). Peter, writing late in the first century, still knows of Jesus' "preexistence" only as an existence in the foreknowledge of God (1 Peter 1:20).

His sermons in the early chapters of Acts reflect exactly the same view. But what of the favorite proof text in John 8:58 that Jesus existed before Abraham? Does Jesus after all confuse everything by saying on the one hand that the Father alone is the "only true God" (17:3, 5:44)—and that he himself is not God, but the Son of God (John 10:36)—and on the other hand that he, Jesus, is also an uncreated being? Does he define his status within the recognizable categories of the Old Testament (John 10:36; Ps. 82:6; 2:7) only to pose an insoluble riddle by saying that he had been alive before the birth of Abraham? Is the Trinitarian problem, which has never been satisfactorily resolved, to be raised because of a single text in John? Would it not be wiser to read John 8:58 in the light of Jesus' later statement in 10:36, and the rest of Scripture? In the thoroughly Jewish atmosphere which pervades the Gospel of John it is most natural to think that Jesus spoke in terms that were current amongst those trained in the rabbinical tradition.

In a Jewish context, asserting "preexistence" does not mean that one is claiming to be an uncreated being! It does, however, imply that one has absolute significance in the divine plan. Jesus is certainly the central reason for creation. But the one God's creative activity and his plan for salvation were not manifested in a unique created being, the Son, until Jesus' birth. The person of Jesus originated when God's self-expression took form in a human being (John 1:14).10 It is a well-recognized fact that the conversations between Jesus and the Jews were often at cross purposes. In John 8:57 Jesus had not in fact said, as the Jews seemed to think, that he had seen Abraham, but that Abraham had rejoiced to see Messiah's day (v. 56).

The patriarch was expecting to arise in the resurrection at the last day (John 11:24; Matt. 8:11) and take part in the Messianic Kingdom. Jesus was claiming superiority to Abraham, but in what sense? As the "Lamb of God" he had been "crucified before the foundation of the world" (Rev. 13:8, KJV; 1 Pet. 1:20)—not, of course, literally, but in God's plan. In this way also Jesus "was" before Abraham. Thus Abraham could look forward to the coming of the

Messiah and his Kingdom. The Messiah and the Kingdom therefore "preexisted" in the sense that they were "seen" by Abraham through the eyes of faith.11 The expression "I am" in John 8:58 positively does not mean "I am God." It is not, as so often alleged, the divine name of Exodus 3:14, where Yahweh declared: "I am the self-existent One" ('ego eimi o ohn'). Jesus nowhere claimed that title. The proper translation of ego eimi in John 8:58 is "I am he," i.e., the promised Christ (cp. the same expression in John 4:26, "I who speak to you am he [the Christ]").12 Before Abraham was born Jesus had been "foreknown" (cp. 1 Pet. 1:20). Jesus here makes the stupendous claim to absolute significance in God's purpose.

Salt of the earth

An Address to All Who is the salt of the earth? Who is the light of the world? The answer is given in the old English, which is not always apparent in the newer translations. The Authorized Version of 1611 has borne true to the Koine Greek language from whence we translate the New Testament. In Matthew 5:13 it reads, "Ye are the salt of the earth…." Matthew 5:14 reads, "Ye are the light of the world…." The word "ye" is a plural expression meaning "all." In a similar fashion, the Great Commission states, "…Go ye into all the world, and preach the gospel to every creature" (Mark 16:15). We are all responsible to be witnesses in this world. Jesus, looking out over the multitudes of His day, saw the corruption and the disintegration of life at every point. He saw its spoliation and because of His love of the multitudes, He knew the thing they needed most was salt in order that the corruption would be arrested. He saw them wrapped in gloom, sitting in darkness, groping amidst fogs and mists, and He knew that they needed, above everything else, light.

When someone says, "Please pass the salt," we don't reach in the saltshaker and take one grain of salt; we pass a container of the substance. When the Lord referred to us as being the light of the world, He said, "…A city that is set on an hill cannot be hid" (Matthew 5:14b), meaning, it is the collective witness of all of us shining forth into the darkness. Here is another passage where the plural "ye" is emphasized: I Peter 2:9, "But ye are a chosen generation, a royal priesthood, an holy nation, a peculiar people; that ye should shew forth the praises of him who hath called you out of darkness into his marvellous light."

A Craving to Create In Matthew 5:13a, Jesus said, "Ye are the salt of the earth…." Salt, from ancient days until now, was and still is primarily used to flavor food. Christians have God within them and therefore, like salt changes the flavor of food, we influence our environment. Job 6:6 asks, "Can that which is unpleasant be eaten without salt? or is there any taste in the white of an egg?" President Woodrow Wilson related an interesting story. He said, "I was in a very common place. I was sitting in a barber chair when I became aware that a personality had entered the room. A man had come quietly in upon the same errand as myself, to have his hair cut, and sat in the chair next to me. Every word the man uttered, though it was not in the least didactic, showed a personal interest in the man who was serving him. And before I got through with what was being done for me, I was aware that I had attended an evangelistic service, because Mr. D.L. Moody was in that chair. I purposely lingered in the room after he had left and noted the singular effect that his visit had brought upon the barbershop. They talked in undertones. They didn't know his name, but they knew that something had elevated their thoughts. And I felt that I left that place as I should have left the place of worship.

My admiration and esteem for Mr. Moody became very deep indeed." Not only does salt influence, but salt heals. In Ezekiel 16:4, we see God referring to Jerusalem's fallen state by using this metaphor, "…neither wast thou washed in water to supple thee, thou wast not salted at all, nor swaddled at all." Salt was used as an antiseptic for a baby as soon as it was born to address any nicks or scratches that would fester into infection. We see in Scriptures such as II Chronicles 13:5 and Leviticus 2:13 salt is used to symbolize covenant. Christians are in covenant with God and we are to be ambassadors for Christ to help others be reconciled to God and to establish covenant with God through Christ. Salt preserves. Before the days of refrigeration, salt was often used to preserve meat. II Thessalonians 2:7 and 8 point out that when the residency of the Holy Spirit (which is the Church) is removed at the rapture, all iniquity is loosed on the earth. When we lose our testimony and influence for good, Jesus said we are like salt that has lost its savour. We are "…good for nothing…" (Matthew 5:13b). I have read that there are two

things that deteriorate the saltiness of salt: exposure to the elements and too close proximity to the earth. Our Lord wants to keep us in the world, but away from the evil in the world

(John 17:15-17). Too much exposure and too close proximity to the world will not only cause us to lose our savour, "…but to be cast out and trodden under foot of men" (Matthew 5:13c).

Being the salt of the earth is An Assignment to Keep Matthew 5: 14-16, "Ye are the light of the world. A city that is set on an hill cannot be hid. Neither do men light a candle, and put it under a bushel, but on a candlestick; and it giveth light unto all that are in the house. Let your light so shine before men, that they may see your good works, and glorify your Father which is in heaven." The Lord Jesus said, "Then spake Jesus again unto them, saying, I am the light of the world: he that followeth me shall not walk in darkness, but shall have the light of life" (John 8:12). Romans 10:17 tells us, "So then faith cometh by hearing, and hearing by the word of God." The result is found in Psalm 119:130a: "The entrance of thy words giveth light…." Thus we may boldly say with Psalm 27:1a, "The LORD is my light and my salvation…." Since the Lord who is the Light has come into our hearts, we are to do what the children's song of our youth tells us to do: "This little light of mine, I'm going to let it shine!" In Matthew 13:43a we find, "Then shall the righteous shine forth as the sun in the kingdom of their Father...." II Corinthians 4:6 says, "For God, who commanded the light to shine out of darkness, hath shined in our hearts, to give the light of the knowledge of the glory of God in the face of Jesus Christ." people, seeing his face lit up with a hallowed expression, fell on their knees to accept Jesus Christ as personal Savior. We are not to be swallowed up of this present darkness. Jesus used the example that we are to be a city on a hill, not hidden beneath the basket.

Our good works that come as a result of being saved and dedicated to Christ become a drawing point to Christ. Philippians 2:15 reminds us, "That ye may be blameless and harmless, the sons of God, without rebuke, in the midst of a crooked and perverse nation, among whom ye shine as lights in the world." We are to be guiding the way to Jesus! At the end of his life the atheist, Bertrand Russell said in his final statement, "Philosophy has proved a washout to me." We have the answer and when we live in such a way that our lives are "salty," we will make others thirsty for Christ. Then we may assist them with the light we have in Jesus to not only find the Way, but to change the world in which we live. Martyn Lloyd-Jones wrote, "Most competent historians are agreed in saying that what undoubtedly saved England from a revolution such as was experienced in France at the end of the 18th Century was nothing but the evangelical revival. This was not done because anything was done directly, but because masses of individuals had become Christians and they were living this better life. They had this higher outlook. I do believe this book

and the readers will walk in the evangelical revival of our time. You are part of this new move are you ready? On one hand, salt is basically hidden, but on the other hand, light is quite visible. We know from looking at the Scriptures that light is mentioned almost from the very beginning of the Bible. The Bible starts by saying, "In the beginning God created the heavens and the earth. The earth was formless and void, and darkness was over the surface of the deep, and the Spirit of God was moving over the surface of the waters. Then God said, 'Let there be light'; and there was light. God saw that the light was good; and God separated the light from the darkness. God called the light day, and the darkness He called night. And there was evening and there was morning, one day" (Genesis 1:1-4). From there, we can skip all the way to the very last book in the Bible, and in Revelation 22:5 (referring to heaven), the Bible says, "And there will no longer be any night; and they will not have need of the light of a lamp nor the light of the sun, because the Lord God will illumine them; and they will reign forever and ever."

Natural Light source

In our own experience, probably the sun is the brightest light that any of us have ever seen, although you could perhaps make the case that the brightest light is the bathroom light at 3 o'clock in the morning. We know that the sun is nearly 93 million miles away, its light takes more than 8 minutes to get here, and yet we know that just the light from the sun can blister human skin in less than an hour. We know that sun damage can lead to various kinds of skin cancer. The sun is that bright.

The second major source of light here on earth is the moon—reflecting the light of the sun. And although it is nearly 240,000 miles away, the moon has a huge impact on our oceans—causing the tides to rise and fall. Perhaps we have seen another natural light source, the northern lights.

However, closer to earth, we can consider one of many other natural sources of light—the lightning bug or the firefly—a source of fun for children of all ages!

• Of course, since the invention of the incandescent light bulb in the mid 1800's, we have been able to use light in ways that people from the past could hardly imagine.

• We now have traffic lights—although I am very thankful I have never seen anything like this here in Madison.

• The police have lights, and those lights pulling up behind us will normally either make us very mad or very relieved—depending on our behavior.

• We have all kinds of warning lights—lights that tell us to check the oil or take the car in for service.

• We have headlights—keeping us safe as we drive around at night—helping us to see and be seen.

• We have lighthouses along the shore.

• We have surgical lights.

• And maybe scariest of all, there is that light at the dentist!

- After 9-11, we have seen lights used as memorials.

- We have artificial lights used for tanning.

- We can visit the "City of Lights."

- We understand that a light does not have to be huge to be incredibly important.

- We know the importance of a lantern when camping.

- We know the importance of the tiny light that allows us to see what time it is in the dark.

- Astronauts tell us about looking back down at earth and seeing the city lights.

- We are familiar with stadium lights that allow us to see a game played at night.

- We know the importance of lights when it comes to various forms of advertising.

- And then we are familiar with the lights that are used to lure little critters, and we know that it does not end well for them.

- We have seen some beautiful chandeliers, but then again…

- …perhaps there is another light that is more important than anything we have considered—the light that comes on when we open the fridge! Who could do without it?

We live in a world, therefore, that puts a great value on light! I would like for us to consider what Jesus has to say to us as Christians concerning our role as lights in this world. If you will, please turn with me to Matthew 5:14-16. In the Bible, this is what Jesus says in Matthew 5:14-16, "You are the light of the world. A city set on a hill cannot be hidden; nor does anyone light a lamp and put it under a basket, but on the lampstand, and it gives light to all who are in the house. Let your light shine before men in such a way that they may see your good works, and glorify your Father who is in heaven." This morning, I would like for us to consider the value of light, I'd like for us to consider a special danger that Jesus addresses here, and then I would like for us to close with what Jesus says is the purpose for the light that we shine.

The Value of light

Are you afraid of the dark? certainly, we understand that almost any light is most appreciated and most needed in the darkness. We look at the statistics, and we discover a significant number of people in all cultures around the world have at least some fear of the dark. And I would suggest that the rest of us are at least a little nervous—and we know why. There are some pretty good reasons to fear the dark. Of course, this is probably not something we should tell our children right before bed (I certainly do not recommend that), but there are some good reasons to fear the dark.

We know that most violent crimes take place at night or in the dark. I remember living in a community house in Sierra Leone, remember the house has a lamp only is used to keep darkness out, I remember when I was younger and studying with the lamp in an open place with other kids my age at that time and I remember the streets covered with darkness and there was a time the workers or seller of food would have light (lamp made from milk cans) on their table in my community in Sierra Leone. I believe there are others who live in taller buildings with staircases without a single light—no windows and no lights—the stairs were absolutely and completely dark. some who have light and others who don't have light would steal the bulbs, or they would light them on fire, they would smash them with stones, we can hardly imagine a mother lugging her groceries or her kids in a total darkness. And imagine other students who had to find a way or developed a bullet-proof, fire-proof, smash-proof, and theft-proof light fixture. And there will be lesser crime situation in their community and improved life and death rate. It is amazing what light can do to prevent crime in a neighborhood.

We understand what Jesus said (referring to Himself) in John 3:19-20, "This is the judgment, that the Light has come into the world, and men loved the darkness rather than the Light, for their deeds were evil. For everyone who does evil hates the Light, and does not come to the Light for fear that his deeds will be exposed." It is interesting, then, that the Bible sometimes pictures evil in terms of darkness, and in that regard, the world around us is a very dark place. People all around us are living in the darkness of alcohol abuse, and violence, and lying, and stealing, and murder, and hatred, and prejudice, and all kinds of sexual sin. Our society has declared itself free from God—free from moral restraint. Jesus, then, says to us as Christians, "You are the light of the world." As Christians, we are the ones who bring our light into the darkness. Where there is a deep dark understand that even the smallest of lights had a huge impact. And At time if you stand in the dark for too long your eyes adjusted to total darkness, And if you have on a watch with light—even the dim light from a watch will bring brilliant! You could see people's faces by the light of a single watch! Jesus is saying: You as Christians are that light! You are the light of the world! As Christians, then, our lives are on display. Our lives serve as an example of what it means to live the Christian life. As Christians, our role is to open the

word of God and demonstrate the light of God's word in a very dark world. The light of God's word reveals what is dark and sinful. The light of God's word reveals what is hidden. The light of God's word reveals the path back to God.

Back in the First Century, homes often had only one room, and everything a family had could be packed away in a chest or a trunk. They had a little oil lamp, and that oil lamp would be kept on top of that chest. That chest served as their kitchen, it served as their table, it served as their place to get together as a family—and that lamp was always there on the table right there in the middle of the room, and that little lamp would light up the whole room. As Christians, then, we are like that little lamp. As the light of the world, we are responsible for leading people back to God. As Paul said in Philippians 2:14-15 (and as brother Stuart read for us earlier), "Do all things without grumbling or disputing; so that you will prove yourselves to be blameless and innocent, children of God above reproach in the midst of a crooked and perverse generation, among whom you appear as lights in the world." First of all, then, we see the value of light, because as Christians, we bring light to a very dark world through our example.

Christian Light

The danger comes in the temptation to hide our Christian light. Jesus gives two illustrations. First of all, He refers to the fact that, "A city set on a hill cannot be hidden." I think we've all been driving at night and have seen the lights of a far-off city. Perhaps you have had the experience of flying over the ocean. I remember how excited it was when I was coming to America and flying over the Atlantic, to stare out into the darkness for hours and hours, and then to suddenly see those city lights in New York. The light of a city can hardly be hidden. Those lights are very easy to notice in a sea of darkness.

Jesus goes on to say "Nor does anyone light a lamp and put it under a basket." What a ridiculous picture that is! Think about a darkroom technician, sealing light out of a room, and discovering through experience is that aluminum foil is great at blocking light. And so even if you had a window in a room, you could cover that window with foil, and it would completely seal out any light. But whether we use foil or a bushel basket, it makes no sense to turn on a light and then immediately cover it up—it defeats the purpose of the light! Nevertheless, Jesus appears to say that covering up our light is a real temptation.

Well, how would this express itself? What would this look like in the average Christian? One way we might cover up our Christian light is by separating our spiritual lives from the rest of our lives. There are two type of life style:

(worldly Christian who only go to church to show their faces)

(there are those Christians who fast and pray and live a life of holiness and righteousness before our Lord and savior)

We must also know that there is level of fasting and praying that is needed to stand strong. It is so easy to divide our lives into categories—we have school, and family, and work, and recreation, and then over here (separate and apart from these others) we have our spiritual lives. And so, if I am at work, then that is not a spiritual situation, and I'd better keep quiet. If I am at school, then I can create a barrier there, and I can prevent the influence of my secular life by anything from the spiritual category. But the Lord would say that our Christian light should shine in every situation, in every category. Our Christian influence is not something that we can cover up, but it is always on.

Another strong temptation here is to simply huddle together as Christians to the point where we no longer interact with the world. And certainly, it is great to be together as Christians, and we should not miss a minute of that fellowship, but let us not be with each other to the exclusion of interacting with people in the world around us. Studies have suggested that when someone becomes a Christian, that person will no longer have any close friends who are not Christians within a period of about three years. And again, we love being with each other, and that is good, but let us not neglect our relationships with those who are lost. Jesus would compare that to covering up a lamp with a basket. After all, Jesus had friends who were sinful people, and He regularly got together and ate with those who were tax collectors, drunks and sinners. We may be tempted to only spend our time with other Christian people, but Jesus, I believe, would encourage us to get out there and live!

There is another temptation that affects our Christian influence, and it goes back to just about any sin we could possibly commit. We can cover up our Christian light by lying, by committing any kind of sexual sin, by living with jealousy and envy— whatever it is, if we continue in sin, people notice that, and we lose our Christian influence. One of the qualities of light is that light is very different from darkness. And so if people in the world lie, and we lie, there's no light there—there is no difference. If people in the world cheat on their spouses and get divorced, and if we do the same

thing, we are no longer different, and we have lost our ability to light the way. If people in the world do a sloppy job at work and always complain against the supervisors, and if we do the same thing, we have lost our Christian influence.

And so we have the category problem, we have the holy huddle problem, and we have the broken influence problem—all of these things have the potential of putting a basket over our Christian light. Jesus, though, would remind us that there is no on and off switch, but the light is to be on all the time. Some of us are the only light that some people will ever see—we are the city set on a hill which cannot be hidden. As far as I know, the Bible does not allow someone to be an undercover Christian. But our Christian faith shows in how we treat the clerk at the store, in the way we order a meal at a restaurant, in the way we react to inconveniences, in the way we serve our employees, in the way we dig a trench, in the way we treat the UPS driver (always say thank you my daughter and son always so thank you) , in the way we drive a forklift, and even in the way we drive our car home from work when the day is over. Jesus never told us to be the light of the church, but He told us that we are the light of the world. We may get discouraged and think that our little light won't make a difference, but as we learned from that watch-light in the cave, even a little light can go a long way in a very dark place. We notice, then, that there is a special danger in keeping our light hidden.

LETTING OUR LIGHT SHINE

Do you see a man skilled in his work? He will stand before kings; He will not stand before obscure men. Prov 22:29

Most of us know what Jesus is about to say and at first it almost seems contradictory—because three times in Matthew 6, Jesus very sternly warns His disciples not to practice their righteousness to be seen by others—especially when it comes to giving, and praying, and fasting. And so it is a little strange to find that Jesus is basically telling us here in Matthew 5:16 to go out and be noticed.

But as with so much of our Christian faith, our motivation is the key. As Jesus puts it in Matthew 5:16, "Let your light shine before men in such a way that they may see your good works, and glorify your Father who is in heaven." In Matthew 6, the Pharisees were praying and fasting so that they would be praised by men, but in Matthew 5:16, Jesus is telling us to let our lights shine so that people will, "…glorify your Father who is in heaven." Our motivation makes all the difference in the world! Our goal in living the Christian life in public is not to glorify ourselves but to glorify our Father in heaven. Our mission is summarized by Peter in 1 Peter 2:9, "But you are A CHOSEN RACE, A royal PRIESTHOOD, A HOLY NATION, A PEOPLE FOR God's OWN POSSESSION, so that you may proclaim the excellencies of Him who has called you out of darkness into His marvelous light." Our goal, then, is to take our light into a dark world so that people will know who God really is. As I was preparing for this book, I ran across a statement apparently made by a Christian in the year 177 AD.

The man's name was Athenagoras, and this is what he wrote concerning the Christians of his time, "Among us you can find uneducated people, artisans, and dear old mothers who would not be able to put into words the usefulness of their teaching, but by their deeds they demonstrate the usefulness of their principles. They do not repeat words learned by heart, but they show good deeds: When hit they do not hit back, when robbed they do not go to court, they give to those who ask, and they love their fellowmen as themselves." That sounds a lot like the Sermon on the Mount, doesn't it? Do the people around us know how we take care of each other? Do our friends and neighbors know what life in the New Testament church is like? The purpose of letting our light shine is to glorify our Father in heaven.

A lot of times people get mad at the light—kind of like what happens when someone drives toward us on the highway with the high-beams on. But let's remember that the darker it gets, the easier people can see even a very dim light, and the more good we can do. It has been said that Benjamin Franklin wanted to interest the people of Philadelphia in street lights. However, he did not try to persuade them with arguments; in fact, he did not even talk about it.

Instead, he hung a beautiful lantern on a long bracket right outside his own front door. He kept the brass polished, and he made sure it was lit every night right before the sun went down. It was not too long before his neighbors started doing the same thing, and soon the entire city saw the value of street lights. The moral of that story is this: If we want to brighten the moral darkness all around us, we start by letting our own lights shine. As the old saying goes, we can either curse the darkness, or we can light a candle.

Carrier of Christ's Light

You are the light of the world. A city that is set on a hill cannot be hidden. Nor do they light a lamp and put it under a basket, but on a lampstand, and it gives light to all who are in the house. Let your light so shine before men that they may see your good works and glorify your Father in heaven."

Matthew 5:14-16

I believe the Lord Jesus Christ, here in Matthew 5, is saying to us, "Join hands. Be salt and light; sweep through the field of the world to find all of those who are desperately in need of your influence and your message." I don't think one or two can do it. I don't even think a handful can do it. I think the whole church has to join hands and be collective salt. Salt is useless as far as one grain is concerned, and light is a combination of fluorescence. We've got to take hands and sweep through the world, and that's the message that Jesus is giving us right here. We are salt and light to reach the lost with the Gospel of Jesus Christ, and this is the vital message contained in our Lord's words. He has followed up the Beatitudes.

In the Beatitudes, He says, "Here is the character I expect you to have, and if you have this kind of character, then you are a child of My Kingdom.

If you have this character, and are a child of my Kingdom, here is your job: sweep through the world as salt and light and make a difference." Jesus is calling on us, to influence the world for His glory, to find the lost before it's too late. The key is what has gone on in the verses before. Having magnificently come to know the principles and the qualities that render us effective for God, that bring us into His Kingdom, that make us distinct from the world, He now tells us, "Move out into the world with that marvelous distinctiveness, find those that are lost, and bring them to Christ." The supreme matter in the Kingdom is character; character is the issue. The character described in the Beatitudes makes it possible for us to affect the world.

You know, I really worry a lot in my own heart about Church and Churchs in this regard.

I think we can get to the place where we are so in love with each other, if you will, where we are so thrilled about everything that goes on here. We can be so happy about it all, and sit in little groups and disciple each other, pray with each other, counsel each other, talk to each other, but the fact is, we're always in danger that we won't link hands and sweep through the world.

We are in danger of never crawling out of our ivory tower of the bliss of our Christian fellowship.

The Lord is saying that's something that we have to do.

The emphatic is here - we are the only salt and we are the only light the world will ever know.

To better understand this concept, let's examine what Jesus meant when he said, "You are the light of the world!"

   1.First, Light is something which is meant to be seen!

• Without a guiding light, you will get lost.

• So the primary duty of the light of the lamp is to be seen.

• So, then, Christianity is something which is meant to be seen.

 • There is no such thing as secret discipleship.

• Our faith in Jesus should be perfectly visible to all, both within and without the church.

• Our light should be seen in the ordinary activities of everyday life.

   • The way we treat people in the work place, the way we treat our fellow coworkers, the way we treat our families, the way we play games, the way we drive our cars, the way we speak…
   • We are the light of the world in the factory, the market place, the school, and our families.

• Jesus did not say, "You are the light of the church!" He said we you are the light of the world!" and our faith in Jesus is to be seen in everyday life.

   2. Next, a light is a guide!

• On the estuary of any river we may see the line of lights which marks the channel for ships to sail in safety.

• On the shoreline of great ports are famous lighthouses, shining their light to guide the ships safely along the shores.

• A light is something to make the way clear.

• So too we as Christians must of necessity be a guiding light, a living example.

• One of the things the world desperately needs more than anything else is people who are prepared to be the guiding light for others.

• There are many people in this world who do not have the moral strength to take a stand by themselves…but if someone gives them a lead, they will follow; if they have someone strong enough to lean on they will do the right thing.

• It is our duty and responsibility to take the stand which the weaker brother will support, to give the lead which those with less courage will follow.

• The world needs its guiding lights and Jesus said, "You are the light of the world."

3. A light can often be a warning light!

• Warning lights signal danger ahead! Caution! Slow down! Watch out!

• It is sometimes our duty to bring to our children, our friends, our coworkers the necessary warnings.

• Teachers and parents and friends sometimes have to say to the ones we love…caution! Slow down! Danger! You are headed in the wrong direction, but we do it with our arms around them…

• If our warnings are given, not in anger, not in irritation, not in criticism, not in condemnation, not in the desire to hurt, but in love, they can be the warning light that keeps them from crashing and burning on the twists and turns in life.

4. Men are to see our good deeds!

• And what are our good deeds? o Good deeds are simply the love of God practiced in everyday life…good deeds are all acts of compassion, mercy, kindness, and sacrifice.

1. The Bible repeatedly exhorts us to let our good deeds shine o Ephesians 2:8 says, "We are created in Christ to do the good works Christ has pre-ordained for us to do!

2. James says in Chapter 2 – Faith in Christ and Love in Action go hand in hand!

3. Good works can be as simple as driving a friend to the Dr. appointment.

4. Good works is mowing a neighbor's lawn when they can't mow it themselves. o Good works is visiting the sick and elderly

5. Good works is visiting those in prison –

6. Good deeds that Jesus has in mind require love in action that includes some kind of sacrifice on our part!

7. Sacrifice and service move people! ! They melt people ! They stop people in their tracks and make them ask, "Why?" Why would you go out of your way for me? ! What would motivate you to put my interests before your own? ! Sacrificial acts are rarely forgotten ! Sacrifices impact people for a lifetime.

5. Our good deeds are meant to draw attention, not to ourselves, but to God.

• The Christian never thinks of what he has done, but of what God has enabled him to do.

• He never seeks to draw attention to himself, but always to direct the attention to God.

• We must shine with the reflection of God's light.

• The radiance which shines from us is lit by the presence of Christ and the Holy Spirit within our hearts!

• When we allow the Holy Spirit to shine through us to a darkened world, the radiance of Christ shines…the darkness cannot overcome it! And ultimately God is glorified as human hearts are moved by God's love and sacrifice in Jesus Christ.

And finally – The incentives for living as salt and light are three fold…

1. This is the way we ourselves will be blessed!

2. This is the way the world will be best served!

3. And third, this is the way God will be glorified.

• Right at the beginning of Jesus' ministry Jesus tells us that if we let our light shine so that our good works are seen, our Father in heaven will be glorified!

• At the end of his ministry, in the upper room, he expresses the same truth: "By this my Father is glorified, that you bear much fruit, and so prove to be my disciples." (Jn 15:8).

• This is the grand purpose and desirability of the Christ-life and the Christian counter-culture.

• It brings blessings in ourselves, salvation to others, and ultimately glory to God."

YOU ARE THE LIGHT OF THE WORLD!

This is precisely why we need to be Born again and FILLED WITH THE HOLY SPIRIT! –
So we can be shining stars of the light of Jesus Christ in a darkened world!

So let me ask you – have you accepted Jesus Christ as your personal savior?
Have you made the wonderful discovery of the Spirit filled life.

YE ARE

to open their eyes, so that they may turn from darkness to light and from the power of Satan to God, that they may receive forgiveness of sins and an inheritance among those sanctified by faith in Me.' Acts 26:18

To one there is given through the Spirit the message of wisdom, to another the message of knowledge by the same Spirit, 1 Corinthians 12:8

If you forgive anyone, I also forgive him. And if I have forgiven anything, I have forgiven it in the presence of Christ for your sake, 2 Corinthians 2:10

Ye are the light of the world. A city that is set on an hill cannot be hid. Matthew 5:14

A. Light Revealed

So, God loves man so much, and wants to help people in darkness to see His light, so He deposited the light in:

- The Scripture – Psalms 119:105

Psalms 119:105 105 Thy word is a lamp unto my feet, and a light unto my path.

- The Saviour – John 9:5

John 9:5 5 As long as I am in the world, I am the light of the world.

B. Light Received

- Believing

John 12:35-36 35 Then Jesus said unto them, Yet a little while is the light with you. Walk while ye have the light, lest darkness come upon you: for he that walketh in darkness knoweth not whither he goeth. 36 While ye have light, believe in the light, that ye may be the children of light. These things spake Jesus, and departed, and did hide himself from them.

John 12:46 46 I am come a light into the world, that whosoever believeth on me should not abide in darkness.

- Following

John 8:12 12 Then spake Jesus again unto them, saying, I am the light of the world: he that followeth me shall not walk in darkness, but shall have the light of life.

- Sharing

2 Corinthians 4:3-6 3 But if our gospel be hid, it is hid to them that are lost: 4 In whom the god of this world hath blinded the minds of them which believe not, lest the light of the glorious gospel of Christ, who is the image of God, should shine unto them. 5 For we preach not ourselves, but Christ Jesus the Lord; and ourselves your servants for Jesus' sake. 6 For God, who commanded the light to shine out of darkness, hath shined in our hearts, to give the light of the knowledge of the glory of God in the face of Jesus Christ.

There are many styles of light today:

- Christmas Lights

1. Used only one time a year

2. Used only on a special occasion

3. More for show than anything else

4. As is it is with some Christians today – they come to church once a year or on a special occasion

- Flashing Lights

1. They are on and off – on and off – on and off

2. They have no consistency

3. Some today can't be counted on they are on and off – cold and hot.

- Flash Lights

1. Very useful in a time of trouble, but not all the time

2. Very short life of usefulness

3. Begin to fade out slowly

- Some today are like flashlight,

    1. Flashlight: they're bright as long their batteries are fresh but when their batteries weaken they become dim and when their batteries die, they are of no use.
    2. They have to be charged up all the time.

- Candle Light

    1. Affected by the wind

    2. Good on the inside only

- Spot Light

    1. Can only concentrate on one area
    2. A spotlight (or follow spot) is a powerful stage lighting instrument which projects a bright beam of light onto a performance space.
    3. Spotlights are controlled by a spotlight operator who tracks actors around the stage.

- Flood Light

    1. They cover a wide area, with usually a softer light.
    2. Floodlights are broad-beamed, high-intensity artificial lights.

3. They are often used to illuminate outdoor playing fields while an outdoor sports event is being held during low-light conditions.
4. More focused kinds are often used as a stage lighting instrument in live performances such as concerts and plays.

- Beacon Light

   1. These warn of danger and guide people the right way

   2. a signal fire commonly on a hill, tower, or pole

   3. a lighthouse or other signal for guidance

   4. a radio transmitter emitting signals to guide aircraft

   5. a source of light or inspiration

   6. a guiding or warning light or fire on a high place

   7. a radio station that sends out signals to guide aircraft

   8. someone or something that guides or gives hope to others

   9. Warning Red, Yellow and Green

SHINE BEFORE MEN

Let your light so shine before men, that they may see your good works, and glorify your Father which is in heaven. Matthew 5:16 16

For God, who said, "Let light shine out of darkness," made his light shine in our hearts to give us the light of the knowledge of God's glory displayed in the face of Christ. 2 Corinthians 4:6

Then God said, "Let there be light"; and there was light. Genesis 1:3

A. The Requirements Purpose – Let your light so shine before men

To be a guiding light

Acts 13:46-47 46 Then Paul and Barnabas waxed bold, and said, It was necessary that the word of God should first have been spoken to you: but seeing ye put it from you, and judge yourselves unworthy of everlasting life, lo, we turn to the Gentiles. 47 For so hath the Lord commanded us, saying, I have set thee to be a light of the Gentiles, that thou shouldest be for salvation unto the ends of the earth.

Acts 26:16-18 16 But rise, and stand upon thy feet: for I have appeared unto thee for this purpose, to make thee a minister and a witness both of these things which thou hast seen, and of those things in the which I will appear unto thee; 17 Delivering thee from the people, and from the Gentiles, unto whom now I send thee, 18 To open their eyes, and to turn them from darkness to light, and from the power of Satan unto God, that they may receive forgiveness of sins, and inheritance among them which are sanctified by faith that is in me.

Philippians 2:15-16 15 That ye may be blameless and harmless, the sons of God, without rebuke, in the midst of a crooked and perverse nation, among whom ye shine as lights in the world; 16 Holding forth the word of life; that I may rejoice in the day of Christ, that I have not run in vain, neither laboured in vain.

To be a reproving light

John 3:19-21 19 And this is the condemnation, that light is come into the world, and men loved darkness rather than light, because their deeds were evil. 20 For every one that doeth evil hateth the light, neither

cometh to the light, lest his deeds should be reproved. 21 But he that doeth truth cometh to the light, that his deeds may be made manifest, that they are wrought in God.

Ephesians 5:13 But all things that are reproved are made manifest by the light: for whatsoever doth make manifest is light.

To be a reflecting light

For ye were sometimes darkness, but now are ye light in the Lord: walk as children of light: Ephesians 5:8

B. The Requirements Plan – That they may see your good works

Good works

Titus 2:7 7 In all things shewing thyself a pattern of good works: in doctrine shewing uncorruptness, gravity, sincerity,

Titus 2:14 14 Who gave himself for us, that he might redeem us from all iniquity, and purify unto himself a peculiar people, zealous of good works.

Titus 3:8 8 This is a faithful saying, and these things I will that thou affirm constantly, that they which have believed in God might be careful to maintain good works. These things are good and profitable unto men.

Ephesians 2:10 10 For we are his workmanship, created in Christ Jesus unto good works, which God hath before ordained that we should walk in them.

"GLORIFY YOUR FATHER"

Matthew 5:16 16 Let your light so shine before men, that they may see your good works, and glorify your Father which is in heaven.

One result of our light shining is the Evangelization of men.

We cannot be effective in reaching the lost if our light is not shining in such a way that they can see it.

Though this is a positive it's not the priority. The goal of our good works being seen is so that they may glorify your Father which is in Heaven!

You don't turn a light on to draw attention to the light, but to whatever it is shining on.

Matthew 6:1-4 1 Take heed that ye do not your alms before men, to be seen of them: otherwise ye have no reward of your Father which is in heaven. 2 Therefore when thou doest thine alms, do not sound a trumpet before thee, as the hypocrites do in the synagogues and in the streets, that they may have glory of men. Verily I say unto you, They have their reward. 3 But when thou doest alms, let not thy left hand know what thy right hand doeth: 4 That thine alms may be in secret: and thy Father which seeth in secret himself shall reward thee openly.

The purpose of the light is to illuminate our Father which is in Heaven.

1 Peter 2:12 12 Having your conversation honest among the Gentiles: that, whereas they speak against you as evildoers, they may by your good works, which they shall behold, glorify God in the day of visitation.

1 Peter 4:11 11 If any man speak, let him speak as the oracles of God; if any man minister, let him do it as of the ability which God giveth: that God in all things may be glorified through Jesus Christ, to whom be praise and dominion for ever and ever. Amen.

1 Peter 5:11 11 To him be glory and dominion for ever and ever. Amen.

Ephesians 3:21 21 Unto him be glory in the church by Christ Jesus throughout all ages, world without end. Amen.

Close:

1. To be the light of the world, we must know the light of Jesus Christ as our Savior.

2. To be light in this world is a great privilege and a great responsibility!

3. To those here who have never trusted Christ as their Savior, the invitation is to come and trust the Saviour today.

4. To those who are Christians today the invitation is decided or determine to let you light shine.

5. We are compared to a city that's set on a hill.

Matthew 5:14 14 Ye are the light of the world. A city that is set on an hill cannot be hid.

To those who have dim, darkened or hidden lights may we allow the Lord to do a work in our hearts so that our lives as well as others will glorify our Father which is Heaven.

The Characteristics of Light

The people who walk in darkness Will see a great light; Those who live in a dark land, The light will shine on them. Isaiah 9:2

Then the moon will be abashed and the sun ashamed, For the LORD of hosts will reign on Mount Zion and in Jerusalem, And His glory will be before His elders. Isaiah 24:23

In that day the LORD of hosts will become a beautiful crown And a glorious diadem to the remnant of His people; Isaiah 28:5

Light is one of the characteristics of our Lord. God is light, and in Him is no darkness at all. Jn.8:12 – Then spake Jesus again unto them, saying, I am the light of the world: he that followeth me shall not walk in darkness, but shall have the light of life. As believers we know that we are to be like our Lord. If we are to represent Him as we should, then we must show forth His light. As we continue our study I want to consider the details Jesus reveals as we think on: The Light of the World.

This Light is Personal –

Ye are the light of the world. A city that is set on an hill cannot be hid. We have the light within us; we are the channel by which the light is revealed. Every born again believer has a light that needs to shine. Jesus doesn't reveal that we have potential for light; He declares that we are the light of the world! II Cor.4:6- For God, who commanded the light to shine out of darkness, hath shined in our hearts, to give the light of the knowledge of the glory of God in the face of Jesus Christ. Phil.2:15 – That ye may be blameless and harmless, the sons of God, without rebuke, in the midst of a crooked and perverse nation, among whom ye shine as lights in the world; 1 Thes.5:5 – Ye are all the children of light, and the children of the day: we are not of the night, nor of darkness.

a. Much of the darkness we face today is a result of Christians who have failed to let their light shine. Would you not agree that society is worse morally today than it was ten years ago? What has happened? It is simple, we have failed in letting our light shine and standing for truth! We have an obligation to this world and our Lord to shine for Him.

b. We all have unique opportunities to shine for Jesus. Each of us is around those who need the light of Christ. It is likely that if your light doesn't shine then they will have no light.

c. I can let my light shine, but I can't let your light shine. Many times we have an effect on each other. When our light grows dim, then others tend to allow theirs to grow dim also. The truth is the church has failed in providing light to a dark world. There are enough professing Christians to make a difference. There is an urgent need as never before in our day to be a light for Christ!

This Light is Powerful

– Ye are the light of the world. The church is to be the channel of Light to this dark world. The light shines through us, but we are not the source of that Light. We are merely the instrument, the bulb or candle that reveals the light. Jesus is the Light of men.

1. We have been given the light of Christ. What a powerful light that is. It is able to conquer the darkness of sin. There is no darkness so dark that light can't conquer. A single match in a dark room will dispel the darkness.

2. Do you remember the time that you walked in darkness and the light of Christ opened your eyes that you could see? There is no greater power in all of creation than the power of Christ. His power is revealed through His light.

3. There is a world that slips further into the grip of sin each year. They are deceived and desperately need the light of Christ in their lives. He can take a life that is gripped by sin and make it whole again. We have the power of God within us and there is nothing that can hinder us from letting our light shine. This world has tried for thousands of years, but the Light remains.

This Light is Projected

– A city that is set on an hill cannot be hid. [15] Neither do men light a candle, and put it under a bushel, but on a candlestick; and it giveth light unto all that are in the house. When light is being produced, it cannot be removed; it can only be covered or shut out. I can flip the switch and turn off the light, but as long as it is on, I can do nothing to remove the light. Light has properties that cause it to radiate all around its source.

Light moves at an incomprehensible speed of 186,000 miles per second. That speed could circle the earth 7 times in one second. The light of Christ has the same properties. It cannot be contained. When it is revealed it radiates from the source, touching all that it comes in contact with. It has the ability to penetrate the darkness of the heart and illuminate the soul.

1. The light of Christ needs to be shared with the world. Light is made to shine rather than to be hidden. Jesus implies that it would be foolish to light a candle and then put it under a bushel basket. We are all filled with light, so why doesn't it find its way out into the world. Sadly we have hidden our light. That is the only possible solution. Jesus has placed it in our hearts; we can't flip the switch and turn it off, so it must be covered or shut out. We have made the conscious decision to hide our light.

2. If the light of all Christians were revealed, the entire world would be filled with light. The church is to be that city set upon a hill, revealing light. The world is powerless to stop the light when it is shining. Consider a world so filled with light that when sinners came out of their dark places of hiding that the light immediately exposed them.

3. There is little light being shone and plenty of hiding places, even in the open, for sin. We as God's people need to resolve in our hearts to fill the communities around us with the light of Christ! Darkness will have to flee from the light. We can send Satan and his evil influence packing.

4. Quickly before we move on, I have always loved the illustration that Jesus used concerning hiding the candle under a bushel, or a basket. In Luke 8:16 He refers to placing the light under a bed. No man, when he hath lighted

a candle, covereth it with a vessel, or putteth it under a bed; but setteth it on a candlestick, that they which enter in may see the light. What is the great significance of these two illustrations? Those who hide their light under a bushel are often too busy with the cares and labors of this life for their light to shine effectively. Those who put their light under a bed are so consumed with the pleasures and comforts of this life to let their light shine. I don't ever want to be too busy or comfortable to let my light shine for Him!

I. This Light is Personal (14a)

II. This Light is Powerful (14a)

III. This Light is Projected (14b-15)

This Light is Profitable (16) – Let your light so shine before men, that they may see your good works, and glorify your Father which is in heaven. Our light is not a light of little value. We are to let our light shine that men may see. There is a lost world that would eternally benefit from His light being revealed.

1. The Lord spoke to me as I pondered these verses. I like to get on my "soap box" about the world looking to secular sources for guidance in their lives. Many look to talk show hosts.

2. horoscopes, palm readers, and psychiatrist for answers to their problems. We can rail on them all we want, but the fact is we have let them down. We have the glorious gospel of Christ, the Word of God that has the answer for all of life's problems, and yet we keep it locked away in our stained

glass prisons. There is a world that needs to see the light of Christ. His light serves as a guide for lives.

3. Imagine the chaos at airports at night if there were no runway lights. This world lives in darkness with no guidance from the Lord. His light serves as a warning to those who are lost. It is like a lighthouse for those on troubled seas, or a RR crossing warning of impending

danger. There is a world that is lost and dying, headed for hell that needs to be warned of the judgment to come.

4. His light also brings clarity and reveals truth. There are those who are searching for truth. They are seeking answers to life's questions. The light of Christ can reveal that truth. We have failed to realize what we have been entrusted with. I pray that God will open our eyes to the responsibilities we have and the opportunities we've been given. What this world needs is Jesus. We can share Him with many right around us!

I. This Light is Personal (14a)
II. This Light is Powerful (14a)
III. This Light is Projected (14b-15)
IV. This Light is Profitable (16)

This Light is Productive

Let your light so shine before men, that they may see your good works, and glorify your Father which is in heaven. As men see our light and notice the lives that we live, they are drawn unto the Lord. I remember the day that the light shined in my life. I have never been the same. The light of Christ brought conviction to me as I cried out for salvation.

Mankind is in need of many things, but his greatest need is salvation. It is our responsibility to share the love of Christ with those who are lost. When men see their need for the Lord through the light of Christ, they will come to Him in salvation.

1. You and I have the privilege of being a part of that. If we will only magnify the Lord by letting our lights shine, He will work through us for the good of others and His glory. John 12:32 – And I, if I be lifted up from the earth, will draw all men unto me.

2. Isn't there someone you know who needs the Light in their life? Many are searching for peace in their souls and we can help them find what they need by letting our lights shine.

3. As we let our lights shine for Jesus men will see our good works and glorify the Father. That is an interesting thought. The word works

doesn't emphasize the quality of our works as much as it does their attractiveness, or beautiful appearance. We don't have to be perfect in everything we do as long as we let the light of Jesus shine forth in our lives. Men will notice and it will have an effect.

4. A Hindu trader in India once asked a missionary, "What do you put on your face to make it shine?" With surprise the man of God answered, "I don't put anything on it!" His questioner began to lose patience and said emphatically, "Yes, you do! All of you who believe in Jesus seem to have it. I've seen it in the towns of Agra and Surat, and even in the city of Bombay." Suddenly the Christian understood, and his face glowed even more as he said; "Now I know what you mean, and I will tell you the secret. It's not something we put on from the outside but something that comes from within. It's the reflection of the light of God in our hearts."

A CHRISTIAN DUTY: "LET YOUR LIGHT SHINE."

A personal duty.

1. "Let" - imperative duty.

2. "Your light" - refraction? (John 1:7-9; 8:12)

B. Purpose.

1. It is in the nature of light to shine.

2. It is in the power of light to overcome darkness.

3. There is a need for such light in the world: That others may see God in us and be led to glorify him. Such light has power to magnify God. (1 Peter 2:11,12.) III. HOW SHINE? "So shine," by good works.

A. Naturally.

1. Ephesians 2:10; Titus 3:1; Acts 6:15; 4:19,20.

2. But not ostentatiously. (Matthew 6:1-4.)

B. Willingly and purposely. (Philippians 2:14-16.)

1. Sacrificially - is expensive. (Romans 12:1.)

       3. "The zeal for thy house hath eaten me up." (Psalms 69:9; 119:139; John 2:17.) 3. John beheaded. Jesus crucified. Paul. (2 Cor. 12:15.)

C. Openly - conspicuously - freely.

1. "Before men" - "AS a city set on a hill."

       a. "A letter known and read of all men." (2 Cor. 3:2)

       b. "The gospel according to you." '

       c. "My Mother's Bible."

2. Not always easy. Some "love darkness rather than light, because their works (deeds) are evil."

D. Continuously - not fitfully, spasmodically, or periodically.
1. Luke 9:23; 1 Corinthians 15:58; "Daily;" "always abounding."

Light can never fail you

Because of the LORD's great love we are not consumed, for his compassions never fail. Lamentations 3:22

But He, being compassionate, forgave their iniquity and did not destroy them; And often He restrained His anger And did not arouse all His wrath. Psalm 78:38

He has not dealt with us according to our sins, Nor rewarded us according to our iniquities. Psalm 103:10

    1.   What if we fail? (Ezekiel 3:18.)

    2. In heaven, "Night nor more." (Revelation 22:5.)

    3. When Christianity came the earth was in virtual absolute spiritual darkness: "It was night."

    A. Jesus and his disciples caused a new day to dawn.

    B. Then the church, after a few decades, began to hide her lamp under the bushels of human authority, tradition, and there were one thousand years of night known as "the Dark Ages."

    C. Then Martin Luther and others began their search for the light of God in Christ, revealed in the Bible, and began to dispel the darkness which had become unbearable.

    D. That light was finally found, rescued from the human bushels, and exalted, in the early nineteenth century, by the pioneers of the true gospel as they searched for the ancient order in its divine purity, passed it on to the twentieth century, and is now a great blessing to our generation.

NOT BE HID UNDER THESE BUSHELS.

A. Unbelief. (Hebrews 3:12-19.)

   1. Causes disobedience. (Romans 2:6-10.)

   2. It may be true that -No person believes perfectly, neither does any person doubt completely.

B. Untruth - Ignorance, lack of knowledge, means dark shadows.

   1. Ephesians 4:17-19: "Hardening of their heart."

   2. Shows up in various ways, such as "language of Ashdod," etc.

C. Unconcern.

   1. Negligence. (Hebrews 2:1-3; Revelation 3:15,116.)

   2. Periodical Christianity. (Luke 9:23; 1 Corinthians 15:58.)

Open your Light

The sun will no more be your light by day, nor will the brightness of the moon shine on you, for the LORD will be your everlasting light, and your God will be your glory. Isaiah 60:19

And the city has no need for sun or moon to shine on it, because the glory of God illuminates the city, and the Lamb is its lamp.
Revelation 21:23

There will be no more night in the city, and they will have no need for the light of a lamp or of the sun. For the Lord God will shine on them, and they will reign forever and ever. Revelation 22:5

Openness: characterized by an attitude of ready accessibility about one's actions or purposes

Receptiveness: willingness or readiness to receive - especially impressions or ideas

Once you have committed yourself to achieving your dream, you should begin to notice something rather odd starting to happen in your life: the universe actually begins to help you to achieve it!

You just need to be Open-Minded - that is, you need to be ready and willing to receive what the universe (you might prefer to say God) has in store for you. Some people call this principle the Law of Attraction, but whatever you call it, it is quite true that you will absolutely set in motion unseen forces which will definitely assist you with the manifestation of your dream.

People, events and circumstances will be drawn to you that will actually assist you in the achievement of your dream. You can probably only fully accept this truth when you experience it for yourself; and once you have committed to your dream, you will begin to experience it. Things will start to happen: they may seem like co-incidence at first, but you are now living in an altered reality.

What have you Learned in the first Column? Write three or more things that you may implements in your personal life?

1)

2)

3)

2 Column

He is not the God of the dead, but of the living, for to him all are alive." Luke 20:38

Anyone who is among the living has hope --even a live dog is better off than a dead lion! Ecclesiastes 9:4

The first living creature was like a lion, the second was like an ox, the third had a face like a man, the fourth was like a flying eagle. Revelation 4:7

Wakening your Light

Glorious things are spoken of you, O city of God. Selah. Psalm 87:3

When I was quite young, someone told me, "If you want be really successful, find out what God wants to you to do with your life and then dedicate yourself to achieving it".

the people living in darkness have seen a great light; on those living in the land of the shadow of death, a light has dawned." Matthew 4:16

a light for revelation to the Gentiles, and for glory to Your people Israel." Luke 2:32

So it is said: "Wake up, O sleeper, rise up from the dead, and Christ will shine on you." Ephesians 5:14

At the time, I didn't really like that idea; I did not believe that my life could have any particular purpose; and I did not think that anything God might have in mind would be of any interest to me in any case. Gradually, I have come to believe that what that person said to me, all those years ago, is true.

As human beings, we all share certain basic wants and needs: we have need for food, water, shelter, safety, love, respect and self esteem. We all share an in-built tendency, as Freud stated, to want to move away from pain and toward pleasure. This tendency is part of the human condition for our own good; it keeps us away from harm and generally helps us to make good choices. Most people settle for a pursuing a career that satisfies these basic human wants and needs; and never really think beyond them to what their life could be about.

Somewhere along the line, I came to realise that what God wanted for my life, and what I wanted, were one and the same thing. This understanding came after I had determined to find out what God actually wanted me to do with my life.

It was a profound moment for me. I gradually came to understand my inner hopes, dreams and deepest desires as being implanted by God. So pursuing God's purpose for my life was, in fact, also pursuing my own purpose. When it really came down to it, I finally realised that I needed to look within to discover my own purpose; and once I had found out what it was, it then became possible to dedicate myself to fulfilling it.

So my message to you is simple: it is time for you to wake-up! It is time for you to start thinking of your life in a different way. It is time for you to fulfil your dream - whatever that may be. That is why you are here on the planet right now. By finding and fulfilling your own unique purpose in life you will be living your life to the full.

It is my hope that you will begin to see yourself as a special person, with a truly unique purpose in life - because that is the truth.

BENEFITS OF LIGHT

Glorious things are spoken of you, O city of God. Selah. Psalm 87:3

In that day the LORD of hosts will become a beautiful crown And a glorious diadem to the remnant of His people; Isaiah 28:5

shining with the glory of God. Its radiance was like a most precious jewel, like a jasper stone, clear as crystal. Revelation 21:11

Why let light shine?

A. Necessary for life.
      1. For bodies, plants, living things.
      2. All life depends upon sun's energy.

B. What light does.

      1.   Natural light overcomes, dispels darkness.

      2.   Awakens, cheers, comforts.

      3.   Reveals, heals, determines seasons.

      4.   Makes for health.

      5.   Spiritual light heals, civilizes, guides into Christ

"Now" - "Today." (2 Corinthians 6:2)

Like a lighthouse: Sooner or later it will be the means of saving life, the reason for its existence.

1. Brightly - Clearly - Like a star, reflecting true light.

2. Not timidly.
"The sun of righteousness, with healing..." (Malachi 4:2.)

His light is indispensable for the sinful world.

Individually - Where we are. (Ephesians 4:16; Philippians 2:14-16.)

- "Brighten the corner where you are." (Business, home; society.)
- "Let down your bucket where you are."
- "Acres of Diamonds." (shine where you are)

Commit to your Light

"A man's gift…brings him before great men" (NKJV).
Proverbs 18:16

Do you see a man skilled in his work? He will stand before kings; He will not stand before obscure men. Prov 22:29

Are you pledged to a woman? Do not seek to be released. Are you free from such a commitment? Do not look for a wife. 1 Corinthians 7:27

How miserable those days will be for pregnant and nursing mothers. For there will be great distress upon the land and wrath against this people Luke 21:23

Because of the present crisis, I think it is good for a man to remain as he is. 1 Corinthians 7:26

I wish that all of you were as I am. But each of you has your own gift from God; one has this gift, another has that. 1 Corinthians 7:7

We have different gifts according to the grace given us. If someone's gift is prophecy, let him use it in proportion to his faith; Romans 12:6

There are different gifts, but the same Spirit. 1 Corinthians 12:4

All these are the work of one and the same Spirit, who apportions them to each one as He determines. 1 Corinthians 12:11

What are you doing with your Life: would you say you are living your dream; or are you living from hand to mouth, making the best of things, just getting to the next week - what we might call: existing rather than living?

If you are living your dream, then well done: you are truly on the road to success. If you are not living your dream - or even if you have no dream at present - then do not despair because this little book was written for you. You are going to help yourself to find your dream, develop it and then to actually achieve it!

To live a truly successful life, you do need to first have a dream. As Carl Sandburg, American historian, poet and novelist put it, "nothing happens unless first a dream".

If you think about it, nothing at all that now exists within our experience of physical reality did not first exist in the mind of the person who made it or brought it into being. In all cases, everything is created twice: the physical creation follows the mental creation.

To succeed, you must have a dream, or you may prefer to call it a vision - and you must completely commit yourself to its ultimate fulfilment - that is the essence of the mental creation.

Here is one of the real secrets of success: you should dream big dreams, because you can have anything you want! Read that statement again and let it really sink in because it is true that you can have anything you want; you can be anything you want to be; and you can do anything you want to do. This may at first seem self-indulgent, but remember, your deepest desires were implanted by God.

What does it mean: to commit yourself to your dream or your light? To illustrate, let me tell you a little about the story of Charles Lindbergh. You know, of course who he was - he was the first person to fly the Atlantic solo - nonstop all the way to Paris. An incredible feat which he eventually accomplished in May 1927.

He used to dream of flying the Atlantic during his long-haul flights delivering mail. Once he had imagined the possibility of being the first person to do this, he completely committed himself to its achievement overcoming all kinds of set-backs. He did not allow the negative opinions of the doubters who surrounded him to influence his resolve.

When he was unable to purchase the single aircraft in existence that he calculated would be capable of making that momentous journey, he had his own airplane designed and built. He didn't have the money, but he got a group of St Louis businessmen to sponsor him - that's why the plane was called The Spirit of St Louis - now that's commitment!

Once you have your dream. you too need to demonstrate that kind of resolve - and let me tell you plainly - you are capable of it!

It requires you to take actions that are congruent with your wishes in order to translate them into reality, but the first step is to have that dream - your own dream, not anyone else's ideas about what is best for you in life - and then absolutely commit yourself to its achievement.

Be Persistence to your Light

To those who by perseverance in doing good seek glory, honor, and immortality, He will give eternal life. Romans 2:7

perseverance, character; and character, hope. Romans 5:4

By your patient endurance, you will gain your souls. Luke 21:19

But you know Timothy's proven worth, that as a child with his father he has served with me to advance the gospel. Philippians 2:22

Persistence: refusing to give up, especially when faced with opposition or difficulty; continuing firmly or steadily

Persistence: the act of continually pursuing something in spite of obstacles.

If having a dream and committing to its ultimate achievement is something like plotting your final destination ahead of an exciting journey, then persistence is rather like the engine you need in order to get there.

Persistence is what drives you on to take the next step in your journey; persistence is what prevents you from getting discouraged by what may have happened in the past; persistence is where the rubber meets the road! Here is a story, of unknown origin that illustrates what persistence is all about ... There was a certain man who went to meet a famous guru to ask, "which way is success?" The be-robed, bearded sage did not speak but pointed to a place far off in the distance. The man, thrilled by the prospect of quick and easy success, rushed off in the appropriate direction. Suddenly, there was a loud "splat!". Eventually, the man limped back, tattered and stunned, assuming he must have misinterpreted the message. He repeated his question to the guru, who again pointed silently in the same direction.

The man obediently walked off once more. This time the splat was deafening, and when the man crawled back, he was bloody, broken, tattered, and irate. "I asked you which way is success," he yelled at the guru. "I followed the direction you indicated. And all I got was splatted! No more of this pointing! Talk!"

Only then did the wise old guru speak, and what he said was this: "Success IS that way. Just a little further on than splat!" Translating your dream into an action plan and then constantly taking actions, each and every day, that will move you in the direction of

your goal is what will get you there in the end. No matter how big your goal, you can get there if you will keep your destination in mind and then continually take actions that move you toward the goal.

When you meet an obstacle, as you inevitably will, persistence determines what you will do; whether you will give up or keep going. Persistence is what gets you back on your feet, dusted down and ready to go again.

Your Light in Obstacles

Joshua said, "Why have you brought this trouble on us? The LORD will bring trouble on you today." Then all Israel stoned him, and after they had stoned the rest, they burned them. Joshua 7:25

Then Jacob said to Simeon and Levi, "You have brought trouble on me by making me odious among the inhabitants of the land, among the Canaanites and the Perizzites; and my men being few in number, they will gather together against me and attack me and I will be destroyed, I and my household." Genesis 34:30

then you shall bring out that man or that woman who has done this evil deed to your gates, that is, the man or the woman, and you shall stone them to death. Deuteronomy 17:5

"But as for you, only keep yourselves from the things under the ban, so that you do not covet them and take some of the things under the ban, and make the camp of Israel accursed and bring trouble on it. Joshua 6:18

1 Samuel 14:29
Then Jonathan said, "My father has troubled the land. See now, how my eyes have brightened because I tasted a little of this honey.

It is a sound principle that to become successful, we need to notice what is working and what is not; and be prepared to change our approach in order to get what we want - that is the essence of flexibility.

A wise person once said, "If you always do what you've always done, you'll always get what you've always got". That is a wonderfully true statement - in other words, if you continue doing exactly what you are now doing, then don't be surprised when you don't see any increase or change in your results.

It is the law of cause and effect in operation. The results you are now getting (effects) are the product of the causes (efforts) you have made in the past. To get greater benefits in the future, you need to change what you are doing in the present in order to produce them.

Whilst persistence is an important quality, persistence without flexibility can indeed be futile because, without some flexibility in your approach, you could end up trying to move an immovable object for the rest of your life. The willingness to constantly change what we are now doing and to also demonstrate persistence is what gets us around seemingly insurmountable obstacles.

So notice exactly what is working for you; and notice what is not. Change your approach in some way - you will need to brainstorm various approaches - then continue to observe. By continually changing your approach and finding what works and what doesn't, you will literally become unstoppable.

As an example, consider the story of Kevin Keegan, famous English footballer (soccer) and eventually manager of England. Kevin was told that he would never become a footballer because he was not talented enough, he was not strong enough and he was too small.

It would have been easy enough for him to just give up; after all these people telling him he would never make it were all professionals - surely they should know what they were talking about! What did Kevin actually do?

Well there was nothing he could do about his height, so he worked on what he could do: he worked on his physique until he built a strong, powerful frame; and he worked on his basic ball skills.

If you really want success, in whatever field of endeavour you are pursuing, you can have it - yes you can! But you need to be prepared to work for it - to do whatever it takes. Finding out and then doing whatever it takes is the quality of flexibility.

Faith: acceptance of principles which are not necessarily demonstrable

Faith: strong belief in something without proof or evidence .

There will be many people who will tell you that you will never, or simply cannot, achieve your dream. They are the 80% of people who once had a dream but have now settled for something less. They are the children who once stood in line at school, believing they would one-day become pilots, doctors, actors, singers, ballerinas, missionaries, airhostesses and so on.

But their experience of life gradually ground them down; and their dreams were reluctantly put away. Those dreams still live somewhere, deep down within their hearts, but they no longer believe that they are achievable.

First, their parents worked on them: questioning their abilities, doubting their chances and telling them that they once had the same dreams. Their parents told them they needed to grow-up, be more responsible and life would work out just great.

Then their teachers worked on them: saying that we all have such ambitions, but in the real-world, you needed a trade, a job, a career - and that life had so very few of these exciting opportunities. They ingrained the attitude of the 'scarcity mentality' into their charges - rather than the 'abundance mentality'. They told these children that there just wasn't enough good stuff to go around.

their friends worked on them as they also settled for the jobs on offer, they questioned: what was so wrong with being a sales-person, a plumber, a secretary or a brick-layer? The world needed these tradespeople (and so it does) and there was nothing wrong with making an honest living by providing these services. That was how, gradually, their beliefs about the world were changed - they no longer believed that it would be possible to reach the heights they had once dreamed of - and they made the decision to settle for less; much less.

After all this negative conditioning, only a few of those pilots-in-the making believed they could still learn to fly aircraft; only a few of those singers still believed they were destined to sing for their supper. Many people had their dream literally strangled out of them. And when you are once again ready to pursue what is in your heart, you need to be aware that you are still not immune to this negative conditioning: there will still be very many people ready to tell you why what you are now doing, or about to do, is hopeless!

But, do you know of the work of Masaru Emoto - the scientist who freezes water and takes photographs of its crystal structure? Well, I don't think you could get a more powerful demonstration of the power of faith to impact our physical reality. He has tried a number of experiments which really challenge our conventional ideas about the power of our thoughts

. Amongst other things, he found that water which was frozen when offered a prayer, formed better, more perfect crystals than water which was cursed before freezing.

It sounds bizarre doesn't it, but if our thoughts can do that to water, imagine what they can do to us - we are after all, 75% water! If your thoughts are positive, affirmative and full of faith, then they are transformational. You become literally changed and therefore better able to achieve your purpose - the goal that other people don't think you can possibly achieve.

That's why you need faith - a deep-down belief that, regardless of the evidence, you are going to make it! You are going to achieve what you have set out to accomplish. You are going to make a difference in this life.

Declarations and decrees start at home

Devote yourselves to prayer, being watchful and thankful. Colossians 4:2

Be on your guard and stay alert! For you do not know when the appointed time will come. Mark 13:33

With one accord they all continued in prayer, along with the women and Mary the mother of Jesus, and with His brothers. Acts 1:14

Pray in the Spirit at all times, with every kind of prayer and petition. To this end, stay alert with all perseverance in your prayers for all the saints. Ephesians 6:18

Declarations and decrees start at home. Here are a few to begin declaring over yourself and your family on a daily basis to see your light.

1. I decree by the decree of heaven, that greatness in my life and my household shall be resurrected and made manifest, in the name of Yeshua!

2. I declare and decree that in the remaining weeks and months of this year, that God will answer all of my prayers with UNCOMMON BREAKTHROUGHS, in Yeshua's name!

3. I declare and decree by the Power of the Holy Ghost, every obstacle to my UNCOMMON BREAKTHROUGHS shall be cleared away, in Yeshua's name!

4. I declare and decree whether it is convenient for the enemy or not, my God shall arise this year and my giants shall BE UTTERLY SLAIN, in Yeshua's name!

5. I declare and decree that where the enemy has made any of my program to fail, it will SUCCEED GREATLY, in Yeshua's name!

6.   I declare and decree that the devourer will not consume any of my Ordained Blessings, in Yeshua's name!

7.   I declare and decree that every move the enemy makes against me will be reversed with POWERFUL BREAKTHROUGHS, in the name of Yeshua!

8.   I declare and decree that the OIL OF GLADNESS that the Lord has assigned to my head shall not run dry, in Yeshua's name!

9.   I declare and decree that my mouth shall speak the Living Oracles of God and AWESOME MIRACLES SHALL MANIFEST, in Yeshua's name!

10.   I declare and decree that every day of my life is CROWNED WITH THE BOUNTIFUL GOODNESS OF GOD, in Yeshua's name!

11.   I declare and decree that every power that does not want joy and happiness in my life and my household shall BE SCATTERED, in the name of Yeshua!

12.   I declare and decree that any seat that belongs to me that the enemy is presently occupying, WILL BE RETURNED AND RESTORED, in Yeshua's name!

13.   I declare and decree that any ORDAINED BLESSING that the enemy has stolen shall BE RESTORED FULLY – SEVENFOLD THIS YEAR, in Yeshua's name!

14.   I declare and decree that any pattern of darkness that has enveloped me and my household shall BE UTTERLY BROKEN, in Yeshua's name!

15.   I declare and decree by the Power of God, that MANY DOORS OF OPPORTUNITY and PIPELINES OF PROSPERITY shall be opened unto me in the remaining weeks and month of this year, in the mighty name of Yeshua

16.   I declare and decree that the remainder of this year, my mouth shall BE FILLED WITH UNCEASING LAUGHTER over my enemies, in Yeshua's name!

17. I declare and decree that God shall turn my worst times into my best times before this year is up, in Yeshua's name!

18. I declare and decree that every satanic assignment against my life and family shall BE UTTERLY CRUSHED, in name of Yeshua!

19. I declare and decree that I shall not struggle to be recognized this year, in the name of Yeshua!

20. I declare and decree that God shall announce and promote me, and LIFT ME UP AS A TROPHY OF HIS GRACE in the marketplace this year, in the name of Yeshua!

21. I declare and decree that the voice of witchcraft over my life and household will BE SILENCED AND NULLIFIED, in Yeshua's name!

22. I declare and decree in the remainder of this year, I shall be a candidate for UNCOMMON FAVOR AND BLESSINGS, in Yeshua's name!

23. I declare and decree that THERE IS NO LACK in my life and household because Almighty God, the Great El-Shaddai, the God of Abundance is THE SOURCE OF OUR TOTAL SUPPLY, in Yeshua's name!

24. I declare and decree that THERE IS NO FEEBLE OR SICK PERSON IN MY HOUSEHOLD because THE LORD IS OUR HEALER, in Yeshua's name!

25. I declare and decree that no weapon formed against me and my household shall prosper, in Yeshua's name!

26. I declare and decree that I will not enter into any vehicle or building of destruction, in Yeshua's name!

27. I declare and decree that the Fire of the Holy Ghost will consume all of my stubborn problems, in Yeshua's name!

28. I declare and decree that PROMOTION and PROGRESS and PROSPERITY shall locate me over and over again for the remainder of this year, in Yeshua's name!

29. I declare and decree that all my expectations will be fulfilled, in Yeshua's' name!

30. I declare and decree that the blessing of the Lord will make me EXTREMELY RICH WITH NO SORROW ADDED, in the name of Yeshua!

31. I declare and decree that the Blood of Yeshua will deliver and protect me and my household from all demonic attacks, in Yeshua's name!

32. I declare and decree that THE SHOUTS OF VICTORY AND CELEBRATION JOY shall be heard in the midst of my household daily, in Yeshua's' name!

33. I declare and decree that THERE IS A WALL OF FIRE that surrounds me and my household, in Yeshua's' name!

34. O Adonai Yeshua, my Awesome Miracle-Worker, HASTEN YOUR WORD TO PERFORM AWESOME MIRACLES in every department of my life, according to the Good Pleasure of the Father!

35. O Adonai Yeshua, let the Angels of the living God ROLL AWAY EVERY STONE OF HINDRANCE TO THE MANIFESTATION OF MY ORDAINED BREAKTHROUGHS THIS YEAR!

36. O Abba Father, I thank You for hearing and answering every prayer of mine offered to You in the name of Your Beloved Son, Adonai Yeshua HaMashiach! I BELIEVE AND I RECEIVE THEM RIGHT NOW, in Yeshua's name!

Declarations and activation
of
Light

As I live in God, my love grows more perfect. I can face Him with confidence on the day of judgment because I live like Jesus here in this world (I John 4:17 NLT).

I receive an abundance of grace and the gift of righteousness. I reign in life through Jesus Christ (Romans 5:17).

Wives: As a wife, I submit myself to my husband as is fitting in the Lord. My husband loves me like Christ loved the church and gave Himself up for her (Colossians 3:18 and Ephesians 5:25).

Husbands: As a husband, I love my wife as Christ loved the church and gave Himself up for her. I look out not only for my own interests but also for the interests of others (Philippians 2:4).

Wives: The heart of my husband trusts in me. He has no lack of gain (Proverbs 31:11).

Husbands: I express belief in my wife and encourage her. I have no lack of gain (Proverbs 31:11, 28-29).

Wives: I do my husband good and not evil all the days of my life (Proverbs 31:12).

Husbands: I cover my wife with the Word to present her holy and blameless before the Lord (Ephesians 5:26).

I am kind and tenderhearted to others. I forgive them as God in Christ has forgiven me (Ephesians 4:32).

I can do all things through Christ who strengthens me (Philippians 4:13).

I ask God to set a guard over my mouth. He keeps watch over the door of my lips (Psalm 141:3).

I let the peace of Christ rule in my heart. As a member of one body, I am called to peace and I am thankful (Colossians 3:15 NIV).

I walk in a manner worthy of the Lord, pleasing Him in all respects. I bear fruit in every good work and I am increasing in the knowledge of God (Colossians 1:10 NAS).

I am being strengthened with all power according to His might. I have great endurance and patience (Colossians 1:11 NIV).

God has not given me a spirit of fear. He gives me power, love, and self-discipline (2 Timothy 1:7 ESV).

God loads me daily with benefits. He is my salvation (Psalm 68:19).

I am God's servant and He takes pleasure in my prosperity (Psalm 35:27).

I meditate on God's word day and night. I am successful and prosperous (Psalm 1:2-3, Joshua 1:8).

God makes all grace abound toward me so that I always have all sufficiency and an abundance for every good work (2 Corinthians 9:8).

I honor the Lord with my wealth and the first fruits of all my produce. Then, my barns will be filled with plenty. My vats will overflow with new wine (Proverbs 3:9-10).

I bring the whole tithe into the storehouse. He opens the windows of heaven for me and pours out a blessing so great that I don't have enough room for it (Malachi 3:10).

I prosper in all things. I remain in health just as my soul prospers (3 John 1:3).

God abundantly blesses my provision (Psalm 132:15).

I give and I receive. Good measure, pressed down, shaken together, running over, will it be put into my lap (Luke 6:38).

Jesus Christ is generous in grace. Though He was rich, yet for my sake he became poor, so that by His poverty He could make me rich (2 Corinthians 8:9).

Christ redeemed me from the curse of the law by becoming a curse for me (Galations 3:13 NIV).

I experience all blessings as I obey the Lord my God (Deuteronomy 28:2 NLT).

I am blessed in the city and blessed in the country (Deuteronomy 28:3).

I am blessed from the fruit of my body. I am blessed with today's equivalent of the produce of the ground, the increase of my herds, my cattle, and the offspring of my flock (Deuteronomy 28:4).
My kneading bowl and basket are blessed. It is the means by which I am tangibly increasing (Deuteronomy 28:5).

I am blessed when I come in and blessed when I go out (Deuteronomy 28:6).

The LORD causes my enemies who rise against me to be defeated before my face; they come out against me one way and flee before me seven ways (Deuteronomy 28:7).

The LORD commands His blessing on my storehouses and in all that I set my hand to do, and He blesses me in the land that He is giving me (Deuteronomy 28:8).

The Lord has established me as a holy person to Himself. I keep His commandments and walk in His ways (Deuteronomy 28:9).

All the people of the earth see that I am called by the name of the LORD. Deut 28:10

The LORD grants me plenty of goods, in the fruit of my body, in the increase of my livestock, and in the produce of my ground (Deuteronomy 28:11).

The LORD opens to me His good treasure, the heavens to give the rain to my land in its season and to bless all the work of my hand (Deuteronomy 28:12).

I lend to many nations but I will not borrow (Deuteronomy 28:12).

The Lord makes me the head and not the tail, above and not beneath (Deuteronomy 28:13).

I am my Father's daughter. I am always with Him and all that He has is mine (Luke 15:31).

God blesses me and surrounds me with favour as a shield (Psalm 5:12).

My ways please the LORD and He makes even my enemies to be at peace with me (Proverbs 16:7).

But by God's doing I am in Christ Jesus. He became to me wisdom, righteousness, sanctification, and redemption (I Corinthians 1:30).

The God of hope fills me with all joy and peace in believing so that I abound in hope by the power of the Holy Spirit (Romans 15:13).

The Lord of peace is peace. In every way, He always gives me His peace (2 Thessalonians 3:16).

I always rejoice and pray without ceasing. In everything, I give thanks for this is the will of God in Christ Jesus for me (I Thessalonians 5:16-18).

I am steadfast of mind. He keeps me in perfect peace because I trust in Him (Isaiah 26:3).

The joy of the LORD is my strength (Nehemiah 8:10).

I am confident of this very thing, that He who has begun a good work in me will complete it until the day of Jesus Christ (Philippians 1:6).

God works in me both to will and to do His good pleasure (Philippians 2:13).

I do all things without grumbling or complaining so that I will prove myself to be blameless and innocent. I am a child of God who is above reproach in the midst of a crooked and perverse generation, among whom I appear as lights in the world (Philippians 2:14-15).

I hold fast to the word of life. In the day of Christ's return, I will have reason to glory because I did not run or labor in vain (Philippians 2:16).

I always rejoice in the Lord and my gentleness (graciousness or forbearance) is known to all people (Philippians 4:4,5).

I am anxious for nothing, but in everything by prayer and supplication with thanksgiving I let my requests be made known to God. And the peace of God, which surpasses all comprehension, will guard my hearts and minds in Christ Jesus (Philippians 4:6-7).

I choose to meditate on anything that has virtue or is praiseworthy. I think about things are true, noble, just, pure, lovely, and of good report (Philippians 4:8).

I press on, that I may lay hold of that which Christ Jesus has also laid hold of me. Forgetting those things which are behind and reaching forward to those things which are ahead, I press toward the goal for the prize of the upward call of God in Christ Jesus (Philippians 3:12-14).

The Lord is my God! He is mighty to save. He rejoices over me with gladness and singing. I am quieted by His love (Zephaniah 3:17).

God instructs me and keeps me as the apple of His eye (Zechariah 2:8).

I am a crown of glory and a royal diadem in the hand of the LORD (Isaiah 62:3).

I am no longer called, Forsaken or Desolate. My new names are Hepbzibah (my delight is in her) and Beulah (married). He delights in me and I am married to Him (Isaiah 62:4)!

God rejoices over me as a bridegroom rejoices over his bride (Isaiah 62:5).

The LORD has chosen me for Himself as His special treasure (Psalm 135:4).

I speak God's word and hearing the word increases my faith (Romans 10:17).

I declare God's word about who I am, what I have, and what I can do in Christ Jesus who gives me strength. I am established as His daughter in all ways and I shine in His light (Job 22:8, Isaiah 60:1).

I speak God's word and His angels do the voice of His word (Psalm 103:20).

I speak God's word and it does not return to Him void. His word accomplishes what He pleases and it prospers in the thing for which He sends it (Isaiah 55:11).

I persist in speaking God's word until it accomplishes its purpose. It is like fire. It is like a hammer that shatters a rock (Jeremiah 23:29).

The Lord has given me the tongue of the disciples. I know how to speak a word in due season to those who are weary (Isaiah 50:4).

The Lord God awakens me every morning to fellowship with Him, and He opens my ears to hear as the learned (Isaiah 50:4).

I speak pleasant words that are sweet to the soul and healing to the bones. I am wise and I bring healing (Proverbs 16:24, Proverbs 12:18).

I have a wholesome tongue which is a tree of life to myself and others (Proverbs 15:4, Proverbs 11:30, Proverbs 18:21).

I speak words of life. I am satisfied with the good by the fruit produced by my words (Proverbs 12:14, Proverbs 18:20).

As I speak God's word, He sends it to heal and deliver me from my destruction (Psalm 107:20).

God forgives all my iniquities and heals all of my diseases (Psalm 103:3).

God redeems my life from the pit. He crowns me with lovingkindness and compassion (Psalm 103:4).

God satisfies my mouth with good things and renews my youth like the eagles' (Psalm 103:5).

Christ bore my sins in His own body on the cross and I am healed by His stripes (1 Peter 2:24).

Be Thankful for your Light

Thankfulness: a virtue and a dynamic - activates the Law of Attraction

Thankfulness: a positive emotion involving a feeling of indebtedness

Attitude affects so many things in life. Sales-people are told to maintain a positive mental attitude because it ultimately affects their sales, sportspeople are told to cultivate a winner's attitude because it affects their performance. The laws of success tell us to cultivate a grateful attitude but why should thankfulness affect our success?

It may be difficult, at first, to see exactly how thankfulness, or gratitude, can be such an important key to your success, but by seeking to maintain an 'attitude of gratitude' you are indeed tapping into the timeless laws of success.

Thankfulness is fundamentally related to positivity and negativity. It is so much easier to be positive about your life and the things that are going on in it right now when you are grateful. As A. W. Tozer once commented, 'a thankful heart cannot be cynical'.

The work-place is full of people who are cynical – ready to run the company down, run the boss down and run the industry down; and do you know something, they can, and do, actually produce the evidence that supports their beliefs. Such people are also employing the laws of success; but by talking about what they do not like, they are using the principles to attract what they don't want. Their reality simply reinforces their views about the company, the boss, the industry and whatever else has been the subject of their negativity.

On the other hand, having an attitude of gratitude impacts your countenance and your general outlook on life; and people generally will prefer to work with happy, cheerful, grateful people than miserable, down-cast, merchants of doom and gloom. As a consequence truly grateful people, literally attract opportunities that others miss or even possibly repel.

To help acquire this positive attitude, consider the idea of keeping a Gratitude Journal. Would you, every day for a period of one month, be prepared to actually write down all the things for which you are grateful? You know:

count your blessings, the way you were taught as a child. What do you think might be the result of engaging in such an exercise? Consider the results of this scientific study into the subject.

Two psychologists, McCollough and Emmons, conducted a study on the subject of gratitude and thanksgiving. In the study, three different groups of people were required to keep daily journals. The first group kept a simple diary of all the events that occurred during the day, the second group kept a record of only their unpleasant daily experiences. The final group made a daily list of everything for which they were grateful i.e. the kept a Gratitude Journal.

The results of this amazing study suggested that the exercise of daily gratitude resulted in higher levels of alertness, enthusiasm, determination, optimism and energy. So let it really sink-in ...

• A Grateful Heart Cannot be Cynical.

• Gratitude is Fundamental to Maintaining an Optimistic Outlook.

• The Exercise of Thankfulness activates the Law of Attraction.

Additionally, the gratitude group experienced less depression and stress, was much more likely to get involved in helping others. They also exercised more regularly and made more progress toward their personal goals. Isn't that amazing: just by keeping a Gratitude Journal, the study suggests they were able to positively impact their chances of achieving their goals!

Thankfulness is an attitude and an important key to success. It is an attitude we all need to learn to acquire - particularly when we feel we are in difficult circumstances. So learn to be grateful.

Understand the Passion of your Light

Passion: strong, enthusiastic devotion to a cause, ideal, or goal

Passion: your heart's one true desire or the deepest desire of your heart

It is impossible to think about passion without reference to the heart. Deep within your heart, there is a desire, the pursuit of which will bring you all the happiness, success and fulfilment you really want.

To find your passion is to identify your own unique purpose in life; to live your passion is to achieve the Deepest Desire of Your Heart.

You can achieve whatever you want. You can be the person you were meant to be; and you can really live the life of your dreams.

Those are bold statements but they are true; and more and more people are discovering this wonderful truth for themselves. But if this is indeed true, then why is it that so many people - we think the figure is around 80% - are pursuing jobs and careers they don't really care about?

For our parents and grand-parents, growing up in a world with comparatively few opportunities, it is true to say that their lives were consumed with the whole business of 'making a living' - looking after the physiological and social needs. They worked hard and never really enjoyed the luxury of considering what might be termed the 'higher needs' of the human condition.

Many people in today's workplace are indeed seeking to reach higher and often people think they have reached their peak when they have started to meet their 'esteem' needs, that is, the basic human need for respect, recognition and responsibility. For many people, this means pursuing an interesting career; rather than just getting a job.

However, for very many people, there is still an inner emptiness. Often, this emptiness is experienced more starkly when they have actually

become successful in their chosen careers. They start to wonder exactly what life has been about. The trappings of success: promotion, automobile, house did not bring about the happiness they anticipated. This is a consequence, as Stephen Covey puts it, of climbing the ladder of success only to find when they reach the top that, all along, the ladder has been leaning against the wrong wall.

To really achieve success in life, you must be bold enough to go even higher: to consider what Maslow called. Self Actualisation. This means becoming the person you were meant to be; and living the life you were meant to live. Only by doing this, can you possibly hope to find the true success you really desire. Below are ten steps to walk in your light and the Hand of God unfold in you life.

You must know (be related to) your Source. It is essential that you understand the nature, composition and consistency of your Source, for this is the key to understanding the potency of your potential. If you had a wooden table in your house,

for example, you would be aware that the table is made of wood from a tree. The strength, durability and nature of the table can only be as strong and durable as the tree. If the tree is weak, the table will be the same. Therefore, the potential of the table is determined by the potential of the source from which it came.

The same is true for you. To understand how much potential you possess, you must understand the Source from which you came. You and I possess the qualities and nature of our Source and are capable of manifesting these qualities. We also possess an eternal spirit just like our Source. We will live forever—not because He allows us to, but because it's our nature.

A manufacturer's product must remain related to its source in order to be maintained and supplied with genuine parts and authorized service. Manufacturing companies call this relationship the warranty/guarantee agreement.

This agreement requires that the owner of the product be subjected to the conditions, specifications and operational standards if the manufacturer is to take responsibility for the maximum performance, maintenance and servicing of the product. Violation of the manufacturer's conditions and standards cancels the warranty/guarantee relationship and places the product at the mercy of unauthorized dealers.

The same relationship exists between *God* and *humanity*. God guarantees the maximum performance of our potential if we remain related to Him and submit to the conditions, specifications and standards set by Him. A personal relationship with our Creator is a key to the releasing of our full potential.

2. You must understand how the product was designed to function. Every manufacturer designs, develops and produces his or her product to function in a specific manner. Automobile manufacturers, for instance, design their products to function with gasoline, spark plugs, batteries, pistons, oil, water and so forth. No matter what you do, if you do not supply the elements required for the operational function of the product, it will not perform and maximize its potential.

God designed human beings to function as He does. You and I were created to function by faith and love. These are the fuels on which we run.

The just live—operate—by faith (Rom. 1:17). Without faith, it is impossible to please God (Heb. 11:6). And faith works through love (Gal. 5:6) because God is love, and those who operate in love abide in God and God abides in them (1 John 4:16).

Our potential cannot be released without faith and love. Fear and hatred short-circuit our potential.

3. You must know your purpose. Every product exists for a specific purpose. That reason is the original intent of its existence—the purpose for which the manufacturer made it. Knowing the manufacturer's intent is essential because the purpose for which something was made determines its design, nature and potential.

God created you and gave you life for a purpose. Whatever that purpose is, you possess the potential to fulfill it. No matter how big the dream God gave you, your potential is equal to the assignment. Purpose gives birth to responsibility, and responsibility makes demands on potential.

4. You must understand your resources. All manufacturers provide access to the necessary resources for the proper maintenance, sustenance and operation of their products. Resources and provisions are to help sustain the product while its potential is being maximized.

God, in His great wisdom, provided human beings with tremendous material and physical resources to sustain and maintain us as we proceed in realizing, developing and maximizing our potential. We are never to worship the resources, nor are we to become controlled by them. Idolatry and substance abuse are violations of the Manufacturer's specifications and will lead to the destruction of potential.

5. You must have the right environment. Environment consists of the conditions that have a direct or indirect effect on the performance, function and development of a thing. Every manufacturer specifies the proper conditions under which he or she guarantees the maximum performance of the product. In the manual, the manufacturer will caution against violation of that

specified environment for maximum performance. The right environment is the ideal conditions needed to maximize the true potential.

God created everything to flourish within a specific environment. Plants and animals all need a specific environment in order to live. When the proper environment is violated, the potential for life is disrupted and possibly destroyed. This is also true of humans.

God designed humans to function in the garden of His presence, in relationship with Him, free from sin and in daily communion with His Spirit. Human potential needs this positive environment of fellowship, relationship, love and challenge in order to be maximized. You can never be all you could be in any other environment.

Humanity's fall contaminated our environment and poisoned the atmosphere of our potential. It produced abnormal behavior and the malfunction of the human factor. The key to releasing your true potential is the restoration of God's original environment. Jesus came to restore us to the Father. He sent the Holy Spirit to restore our internal environment.

6. You must work out your potential. Potential is dormant ability. But ability is useless until it is given responsibility. When God created Adam, He planted in him the potential to subdue, rule over and care for the earth and everything in it. His potential was predetermined by this purpose. Adam had inside of him all the potential necessary to fulfill the assignment. But he was not aware of his potential, even as you may not be aware of what you can do.

So the first thing God gave Adam was not a wife, but *work* (Gen. 2:15). He made demands on the potential of Adam's mind by commanding him to name the animals and stimulated the potential of his body by commanding him to cultivate the garden. The Lord gave Adam insight into the potential of his spirit by commanding him to dominate the whole earth for God's glory.

Work is a major key to releasing your potential. Claiming a promise does not make it happen. You must apply the principle of work. The land was promised to the children of Israel, but they had to walk it out to possess it (Deut. 11:24). Good ideas do not bring success. Good hard work does. To release your true potential, you must be willing to work.

7. You must cultivate your potential. Potential is like a seed. It is a hidden ability that needs to be cultivated. You must feed your potential the fertilizer of positive company, give it the environment of encouragement, drench it with the water of God's Word and bathe it in the sunshine of personal prayer. Read materials that stimulate your faith and nourish your dream.

8. You must guard your potential. It's tragic when a tree dies in a seed or a person dies in childhood. It's sad when what could have been becomes

what should have been. With all the wealth of your potential, you must be careful to guard and protect it.

The Bible calls your potential a *treasure* in an earthen vessel (2 Cor. 4:7). You must guard your visions and dreams from sin, discouragement, procrastination, failures, opinions, distractions, traditions and compromise. Satan is after your potential. Be on guard.

9. You must share your potential. God created the heavens and the earth to operate on this principle: Potential can only be fulfilled when it is shared. Nature abounds with this truth. The sun does not exist for itself. Plants release oxygen for us, and we provide carbon dioxide for the plants. The bee receives nectar as it pollinates the flowers.

No potential exists for itself. This is also true of human potential. The true measure of fulfilled potential is not what is accomplished, but who receives benefit from the accomplishment. Your deposit was given to enrich and inspire the lives of others. Remember, the great law is *love*.

10. You must know and understand the laws of limitation. Freedom and power are two of the most important elements in our lives. Potential is the essence of both. Potential is power. But freedom needs law to be enjoyed, and power needs responsibility to be effective. One without the other produces self-destruction.

Every manufacturer establishes laws of limitations. These laws are not given to restrict, but to protect—not to hinder, but to assist and guarantee the maximum performance of potential.

God has set laws and standards to protect our potential and to secure our success. Violating these laws limits the release of your potential. Obedience ensures protection and maximization.

Commit yourself to obeying the Manufacturer. Then watch your life unfold as you discover the hidden ability that was always within you.

Light of Purpose

Success and progress towards achieving your goals in life begin with knowing where you are going. Any dominating idea, plan, or purpose held in your conscious mind through repeated effort and emotionalized by a burning desire for its realization is taken over by the subconscious and acted upon through whatever natural and logical means may be available. Your mental attitude gives power to everything you do. If your attitude is positive, your actions and thoughts further your ends. If your attitude is negative, you are constantly undermining your own efforts. The starting point of all human achievement is the development of a Definite Major Purpose. Without a definite major purpose, you are as helpless as a ship without a compass.

Establish a Mastermind Alliance

A mastermind alliance consists of two or more minds working actively together in perfect harmony toward a common definite objective. Through a mastermind alliance you can appropriate and use the full strength of the experience, training, and knowledge of others just as if they were your own. No individual has ever achieved success without the help and cooperation of others. The value of "gathering together those of a like mind" is self-evident. A group of brains coordinated in a spirit of harmony will provide more thought energy than a single brain, just as a group of electric batteries will provide more energy than a single battery,

Assemble an Attractive Personality

A Positive Mental Attitude is the right mental attitude in any given situation. Courtesy is your most profitable asset... and it is absolutely free! Emotions are nothing but reflections of your mental attitude, which you can organize, guide, and completely control. Your personality is your greatest asset or your greatest liability because it embraces everything you control ...your mind, body, and soul. To be happy, make someone else happy!

Use Applied Faith

Faith is awareness of, belief in, and harmonizing with the universal powers. Faith is a state of mind which must be active not passive, to be useful in achieving lasting success. Close the door to fear behind you and you will quickly see the door of faith open before you. Fear is nothing more than a state of mind, which is subject to your own direction and control. Faith will not bring you what you desire, but it will show you the way to go after it for yourself.

Go the Extra Mile

Strength and struggle go hand in hand. Render more and better service than you are paid for, and sooner or later you will receive compound interest from your investment. The end of the rainbow is at the end of the second mile. The quality of the service rendered, plus the quantity of service rendered, plus the mental attitude in which it is rendered, equals your compensation. The more you give, the more you get.

Control Your Attention

Keep your mind ON the things you want and OFF the things you don't want! It is much easier to focus your attention on something you believe will happen than on something you believe is unlikely. Controlled attention is the act of coordinating all the faculties of your mind and directing their combined power to a specific end. Positive and negative emotions cannot occupy your mind at the same time. Independence starts with self-dependence.

Inspire Teamwork

There is no record of any great contribution to civilization without the cooperation of others. Enthusiasm is contagious and teamwork is the inevitable result. A good football team relies more on harmonious coordination of effort than individual skill. Most people will respond more freely to a request than they will to an order. Helping others solve their problems will help you solve your own.

Learn From Adversity and Defeat

Everyone faces defeat. It may be a stepping-stone or a stumbling block, depending on the mental attitude with which it is faced. Failure and pain are one language through which nature speaks to every living creature. You are never a failure until you accept defeat as permanent and quit trying. Edison failed 10,000 times before perfecting the electric light bulb. Don't worry if you fail once.

Every adversity, every failure, and every unpleasant experience carries with it the seed of an equivalent benefit which may prove to be a blessing in disguise.

Cultivate Creative Vision

Creative imagination has its base in the subconscious and is the medium through which you recognize new ideas and newly learned facts. Synthetic imagination springs from experience and reason; creative imagination springs from your commitment to your definite purpose. Imagination recognizes limitations. Creative vision sees no limitations. Your imaginative faculty will become weak through inaction. It can be revived through use. The man who dipped a chunk of ice cream in chocolate and called it "Eskimo Pie" made a fortune for the five seconds of imagination it took to create the idea!

Maintain Sound Health

To maintain a Positive Mental Attitude and develop a healthy mind and body, you must conquer fear and anxiety. Anything that affects your physical health also affects your mental health. A Positive Mental Attitude is the most important quality for sound mental and physical health. Exercise produces both physical and mental buoyancy. It clears sluggishness and dullness from body and mind. If you haven't the willpower to keep your physical body in repair, you lack the power of will to maintain a positive mental attitude in other important circumstances that control your life.

Budget Your Time and Money

Tell me how you use your time and how you spend your money, and I will tell you where and what you'll be ten years from now. Take regular inventory of yourself to learn how and where you are spending your time and money. The secret of getting things done is: DO IT NOW! Time is too precious to be wasted on arguments and discontent. Some mistakes can be corrected, but not the mistake of wasting time. When time is gone, it's gone forever.

Use of Cosmic Habitforce

It takes a habit to replace a habit. All of your successes and failures are results of habits you have formed. The orderliness of the world of natural laws gives evidence that they are under control of a universal plan. For every result there is a cause, and results are brought about through the use of cosmic habitforce. First you get a habit, then it gets you.

Create Personal Initiative

It is better to act on a plan that is still weak than to delay acting at all. Procrastination is the archenemy of personal initiative. Personal Initiative: is contagious succeeds where others fail creates work creates opportunity creates the future creates advancement Procrastinators are experts in creating alibis. Personal initiative is the inner power that starts all action.

Build a Positive Mental Attitude

A Positive Mental Attitude is the single most important principle of the science of success, without which you cannot get the maximum benefit from the other sixteen principles. Success attracts success and failure attracts more failure. Your mental attitude is the only thing over which you, and only you, have complete control. A Positive Mental Attitude attracts opportunities for success, while a Negative Mental Attitude repels opportunities and doesn't even take advantage of them when they do come along. A positive mind finds a way it can be done... a negative mind looks for all the ways it can't be done.

Control Your Enthusiasm

To be enthusiastic-act enthusiastically! Enthusiasm is to progress toward success, as gasoline is to a car's engine. It is the fuel that drives things forward. Enthusiasm stimulates your subconscious mind. By feeding your conscious mind with enthusiasm, you impress upon your subconscious that your burning desire and your plan for attaining it are certain. Enthusiasm is a state of mind. It inspires action and is the most contagious of all emotions. Enthusiasm is more powerful than logic, reason, or rhetoric in getting your ideas across and in winning over others to your viewpoint.

Enforce Self-Discipline

Self-discipline is the process that ties together all your efforts of controlling your mind, your personal initiative, positive mental attitude and controlling your enthusiasm. Self-discipline makes you think before you act. The subconscious has access to all departments of the mind, but is not under the control of any. If you don't discipline yourself, you are sure to be disciplined by others. Without self-discipline, you are as dangerous as a car running downhill without brakes or steering wheel.

Let your light Think Accurately

Thoughts have power, are under your control, and can be used wisely or unwisely. Accurate thinkers accept no political, religious, or other type of thought, regardless of its source, until it is carefully analyzed. Accurate thinkers are the masters of their emotions. Accurate thought involves two fundamentals. First you must separate facts from information. Second you must separate facts into two classes? The important and unimportant. Accurate thinkers allow no one to do their thinking for them.

Lift Others light

When You Lift up Others, They Will Lift You Up And here's another major benefit—the more you help other people succeed in life, the more they will want to help you succeed. You might wonder why all the people who teach success strategies are so successful. It's because they have helped so many people get what they want.

People naturally support those who have supported them. The same will be true for you. One of my spiritual teachers once taught me to be a student to those above me, a teacher to those below me, and a fellow traveler and helpmate to those on the same level. That's good advice for all of us. One of the most powerful ways to learn anything is to teach it to others.

It forces you to clarify your ideas, confront inconsistencies in your own thinking, and more closely walk your talk. But most importantly, it requires you to read, study, and speak the information over and over again. The resulting repetition reinforces your own learning.

Values are things

Values are things that are personally meaningful to you. To identify your most important values, ask yourself "What do I want other people to remember about me? As I get older, what do I want to be able to look back at my life and be proud of?" For example, some people identify being a good friend as an important value. Others identify religion or spirituality as an important value. Each person has their own set of values, so there's no right or wrong answer to this.

Activity Scheduling

By this point, you have worked on increasing three kinds of activities:

• Enjoyable, pleasant activities

• Activities that fit with your life values

• Activities that give you a sense of accomplishment.

You may have met many of your goals for increasing these three types of activities. To keep yourself moving forward with these changes, we recommend that you make a schedule for working on your goals. This is important for several reasons:

1. Setting a specific time for an activity will help you accomplish it. Otherwise, it's too easy to put off working on your goals.

2. Setting a routine or a schedule can be helpful for following through on your goals. For many people with depression, it can be difficult to get motivated at first. When you have a schedule set ahead of time, you can follow it to help get you moving in the right direction.

Start making a schedule or "to-do list" of goals for yourself today. No goal is too small! Put down everything you want to accomplish, like "cook dinner" or "get the mail." Then check off each goal that you work on.

The Rest of Your Light

You are a truly unique person: you can tell this simply by taking a moment or two to look at your thumb print. Do that now – go on, humour me – take a look at your thumb print and know this: you are the only person who has ever lived who has had that thumb print! Isn't that truly amazing? In fact, it is even more amazing than that because, as it turns out, you are the only person who will ever have that thumb print.

So you already know, in your heart that you are unique. But also know that this uniqueness extends to your purpose in life: you are called to achieve something significant with your life! Do not make the mistake of believing that life holds no purpose for you. Remember that you are here only once. This is your life - right now! So make sure you live the life you were born to live.

Why do I declare? Because the power of life and death is in the tongue (Proverbs 18:21) and whatever I declare and speak in God's ears, He will do to me (Numbers 14:28).

I declare I am loved by my Creator and therefore love myself no matter what anybody else says or thinks about me.

I declare if God be for me who can be against me!

I declare I was born an original and shall not live like a copy.

I declare greater is the Holy Spirit that raised Christ from the dead within me than an adversary or adversity I shall face outwardly within this world.

I declare I have an unction from the Holy Spirit within me that will reveal, teach, and show me all things pertaining to my life and that which I need to know.

I declare I am who the Bible says I am, can do what the Bible says I can do, and will have what the Bible says I can have.

I declare that I walk by faith not by sight.

I declare my faith is a magnet that attracts the blessings of God to me.

I declare God is always doing good things with, in, on, for, through and by me!

I declare I trust with childlike faith my heavenly Father even though I may temporarily may not fully understand all of the details of the miracles God has set in motion on my behalf.

I declare that I am blessed and highly favored of God.

I declare that God is my Source of love, wisdom and power.

I declare that God is my Provider, Financial Adviser and Chief Investor and the deposit He has made in my heart and life will bear much fruit in the earth.

I declare that what belongs to me will come to me as I maintain a pure heart and sensitivity to yield to the Holy Spirit within and work with God.

I declare that no weapon formed against me shall prosper and every tongue that speaks against me shall be silenced and my critics proven wrong.

I declare all adversity is to me a university, making me wiser and stronger.

I declare the sun always shines above the clouds. Therefore I will always remain positive in all things, circumstances and situations keeping heavenly vision and divine perspective.

I declare the best is yet to come as my life has only begun. My days are getting increasingly brighter, more beautiful and more fruitful.

I declare evil people shall not oppress me, thwart my purpose, nor delay my destiny.

I declare divine relationships, blessed alliances, strategic partnerships and creative collaboration for mutual blessing and increase shall continually come my way and be mine.

I declare I will respect and honor myself and every other human being God has made.

I declare I will see people through the eyes of God and not judge them by their past or present circumstances.

I declare my bank account will always be filled to overflowing and my heart burning with passion, purpose and forward progress

I declare I will plunder hell and populate heaven with millions of souls.

I declare I will birth Bible Schools and Churches throughout the earth, 10/40 window and on every continent.

I declare I will revive and reform the nations.

I declare I will win souls and make disciples with the help and guidance of God's Word and Spirit.

I declare I will always give God the glory for all good and great things accomplished by me.

I declare I shall have a dream team to help me fulfill my heavenly calling – a group of people who love me unconditionally, work with me joyfully and compliment my gifts, talents and abilities.

I declare those who bless me will be blessed and those who curse me shall be cursed as I am the seed of Abraham in Christ and an heir according to the promise.

I declare I shall heal diseases, hurts and wounds, remove emotional pain and cause people to be whole body-mind-spirit in Jesus Name!

I declare I will hear the voice of God and value my relationship with my heavenly Father, Christ my Savior and the Holy Spirit above all else.

I declare I will have happiness, health, wealth and lots of time to enjoy them with the people I love and care about.

If you like what I declare and would like me to make some positive prophetic declarations over your life, hear the voice of God (John 10:27; 16:13) and tell you what God shows me concerning you; then invite me to your city to minister and be a blessing to your community. Believe God's prophets and you will prosper (2Chronicles 20:20).

What have you Learned in the second Column? Write three or more things that you may implements in your personal life?

1)

2)

3)

3 columns

And there appeared before them Elijah and Moses, who were talking with Jesus. Mark 9:4

His clothes became radiantly white, brighter than any launderer on earth could bleach them. Mark 9:3

Peter said to Jesus, "Rabbi, it is good for us to be here. Let us put up three shelters: one for You, one for Moses, and one for Elijah." Mark 9:5

The messengers

Zechariah *4:2-12* And said unto me, What seest thou? And I said, I have looked, and behold a candlestick all of gold, with a bowl upon the top of it, and his seven lamps thereon, and seven pipes to the seven lamps, which are upon the top thereof:

- 3 And two olive trees by it, one upon the right side of the bowl, and the other upon the left side thereof.
- 6 Then he answered and spake unto me, saying, This is the word of the Lord unto Zerubbabel, saying, Not by might, nor by power, but by my spirit, saith the Lord of hosts.
- Then answered I, and said unto him, What are these two olive trees upon the right side of the candlestick and upon the left side thereof?
- 12 And I answered again, and said unto him, What be these two olive branches which through the two golden pipes empty the golden oil out of themselves

Zechariah 4:2-12

Revelation 11:3-4

- Revelation 11:3 -4,
- 3"And I will grant authority to my two witnesses, and they will prophesy for twelve hundred and sixty days, clothed in sackcloth. (3year and somedays)
- 4.They are "the two olive trees" and the two lampstands, and "they stand before the Lord of the earth."

What is a Candle

What is a candle: A block of wax with a wick-a strip of absorbent material up which liquid fuel is drawn by passageway stroke to the flame in a candle, lamp, or lighter? Candles are now a common decoration item in homes. Candles are primarily used to create ambiance and relieve stress. However, candles can significantly contribute to the indoor air pollution in your home

Mark chapter 4:21 through chapter 4:23...

21 And he said unto them, Is a candle brought to be put under a bushel, or under a bed? and not to be set on a candlestick? 22 For there is nothing hid, which shall not be manifested; neither was any thing kept secret, but that it should come abroad.

23 If any man have ears to hear, let him hear.

Revelation 22:5 There will be no more night. They will not need the light of a lamp or the light of the sun, for the Lord God will give them light. And they will reign for ever and ever.

- Matthew 5:15 Neither do people light a lamp and put it under a bowl. Instead they put it on its stand, and it gives light to everyone in the house.
- Luke 11:35 See to it, then, that the light within you is not darkness.
- Luke 11:36 Therefore, if your whole body is full of light, and no part of it dark, it will be just as full of light as when a lamp shines its light on you."
- Job 29:3 when his lamp shone on my head and by his light I walked through darkness!
- Psalm 18:28 You, LORD, keep my lamp burning; my God turns my darkness into light.

- Psalm 18:28 For it is you who light my lamp; the LORD my God lightens my darkness.
- Job 11:17 Life will be brighter than noonday, and darkness will become like morning.
- Proverbs 20:27 The human spirit is the lamp of the LORD that sheds light on one's inmost being.
- 1 Corinthians 2:11 For who knows a person's thoughts except their own spirit within them? In the same way no one knows the thoughts of God except the Spirit of God Proverbs 20:28 Love and faithfulness keep a king safe; through love his throne is made secure.
- 1 Kings 15:4 Nevertheless, for David's sake the LORD his God gave him a lamp in Jerusalem by raising up a son to succeed him and by making Jerusalem strong.
- Job 18:6 The light in his tent becomes dark; the lamp beside him goes out.
- Psalm 13:3 Look on me and answer, LORD my God. Give light to my eyes, or I will sleep in death,
- Psalm 27:1 Of David. The LORD is my light and my salvation-- whom shall I fear? The LORD is the stronghold of my life-- of whom shall I be afraid?
- Psalm 118:27 The LORD is God, and he has made his light shine on us. With boughs in hand, join in the festal procession up to the horns of the altar.
- Psalm 132:17 "Here I will make a horn grow for David and set up a lamp for my anointed one.

What is a Wax

Wax –brings heat-sensitive- substances, strength, intensity, (your body can be the wax also) Wax is a generic term for classifying materials that have the following characteristics:

- Solid at room temperature, but liquid at higher temperatures
- Primarily hydrocarbon in structure
- Water repellant; insoluble in water
- Smooth texture and buffable with slight pressure
- Low reactivity, low toxicity and low odor

Waxes can be made from a variety of different materials, including animal fats, insect secretions, waxy plants, vegetable fats and oils, and petroleum-based materials. The majority of today's candles are made from paraffin, beeswax, soy wax, palm wax or stearin, and Wax constitutes the major component of any candle, and accounts for the second largest use of wax in North America (after packaging applications).

wax- progressively large, illuminated area. (Psalms 22:14 ; 68:2 ; 97:5 ; Micah 1:4)

Wax-oily(oil of God)Wax –greasy = Glory of God-Grace of God) Exodus 25:6 olive oil for the light; spices for the anointing oil and for the fragrant incense; Exodus 27:20
"You shall charge the sons of Israel, that they bring you clear oil of beaten olives for the light, to make a lamp burn continually.

Wax or candle is the body and the body of Christ

John 2:21 But the temple he had spoken of was his body.

1 Corinthians 6:19 "Do you not know that your bodies are temples of the Holy Spirit, who is in you, whom you have received from God? You are not your own;"

2 Peter 3:10
But the day of the Lord will come like a thief. The heavens will disappear with a roar, the elements will be dissolved in the fire, and the earth and its works will not be found.

2 Peter 3:12
as you anticipate and hasten the coming of the day of God, when the heavens will be dissolved by fire and the elements will melt in the heat.

Psalm 46:6
The nations made an uproar, the kingdoms tottered; He raised His voice, the earth melted.

Psalm 68:2
As smoke is driven away, so drive them away; As wax melts before the fire, So let the wicked perish before God.

Psalm 97:5
The mountains melted like wax at the presence of the LORD, At the presence of the Lord of the whole earth.

Isaiah 64:1
Oh, that You would rend the heavens and come down, That the mountains might quake at Your presence--

Isaiah 64:2
As fire kindles the brushwood, as fire causes water to boil-- To make Your name known to Your adversaries, That the nations may tremble at Your presence!

Amos 9:5 The Lord GOD of hosts, The One who touches the land so that it melts, And all those who dwell in it mourn, And all of it rises up like the Nile And subsides like the Nile of Egypt;

Nahum 1:5Mountains quake because of Him And the hills dissolve; Indeed the earth is upheaved by His presence, The world and all the inhabitants in it.

Zechariah 14:4 In that day His feet will stand on the Mount of Olives, which is in front of Jerusalem on the east; and the Mount of Olives will be split in its middle from east to west by a very large valley, so that half of the mountain will move toward the north and the other half toward the south.

The body (candle) of Christ are Different people & tribes (color)

The body of Christ is should and will be in order like crayons in the box, with each one in the box has a proposed. We as people in Christ embrace Our cultures which are defined by our likes, dislikes, and worldview. In many cases, cultures are not right or wrong, but simply different. Don't allow differences to become points of conflict or animosity.

Be intentional about learning the cultures of others. Lead your church members to take initiative to value people of different ethnicity or culture by having meals together or going on mission trip. View differences as a learning experience. Become genuinely interested in people who are different than you. some churches have value their race or cultural identity much more than their identity in Christ.

It's a problem that hinders evangelism efforts and it hinders unity within the Body of Christ. The racial and cultural walls of division are massive and are not easily torn down. It's a problem that exists nearly everywhere we turn. Revelation 7:9-10 provides for us a picture of the redeemed people of God gathered and singing before God's throne, "Salvation belongs to our God." They are described as a "vast multitude from every nation, tribe, people, and language, which no one could number, standing before the throne and before the Lamb."

Multitude of nation and tribes as well as Languages are form for One people, one blood, one covering however different coloring.

The Coloring - There are several types of coloring that you may use for candle making. Each type has its pros and cons. experience in candle has concluded the following about each type of coloring or people and tribes.

(a) Color Blocks - Color blocks provide you with the richest and most cost effective means of coloring your candles. Unfortunately, when you choose to use color blocks for candle making it is difficult to achieve color accuracy each and every time. This problem can be resolved by buying a gram scale and weighing your color......but that takes a lot of time, TIME is MONEY. We use color blocks to make our dark colors only.

(b) Liquid dye - Liquid dye provides you with a solution to the color accuracy problem, but all liquid dye had any experience with does have a slight chemical smell to it.

(c) Color chips -color chips are over-priced, and are not finely ground enough to resolve the color accuracy goal.

(d) Crayons - Using crayons to color your candles is not an option for producing high-quality candles! Crayons clog your wick and cause your candles to smoke....forget about using them!

Leviticus 23:40 'Now on the first day you shall take for yourselves the foliage of beautiful trees, palm branches and boughs of leafy trees and willows of the brook, and you shall rejoice before the LORD your God for seven days.

Zechariah 10:8 "I will whistle for them to gather them together, For I have redeemed them; And they will be as numerous as they were before.

Luke 21:36 So keep watch at all times, and pray that you may have the strength to escape all that is about to happen and to

stand before the Son of Man."

Revelation 3:4 But you do have a few people in Sardis who have not soiled their garments, and because they are worthy,

they will walk with Me in white.

Revelation 5:9 And they sang a new song: "Worthy are You to take the scroll and open its seals, because You were slain, and by Your blood You purchased for God those from every tribe and tongue and people and nation.

Revelation 6:11 Then each of them was given a white robe and told to rest a little while longer, until the full number of their fellow servants, their brothers, were killed, just as they had been killed.

Revelation 7:8 from the tribe of Zebulun twelve thousand, from the tribe of Joseph twelve thousand, and from the tribe of Benjamin twelve thousand.

Revelation 7:13 Then one of the elders addressed me: "These in white robes," he asked, "who are they, and where have they come from?"

Revelation 7:14 "Sir," I answered, "you know." So he replied, "These are the ones who have come out of the great tribulation; they have washed their robes and made them white in the blood of the Lamb.

Revelation 7:15 For this reason, 'They are before the throne of God and serve Him day and night in His temple; and the One seated on the throne will spread His tabernacle over them.

After this I looked, and there before me was a great multitude that no one could count, from every nation, tribe, people and language, standing before the throne and before the Lamb. They were wearing white robes and were holding palm branches in their hands. Revelation 7:9

Matthew 19:28 Jesus said to them, "Truly, I say to you, in the new world, when the Son of Man will sit on his glorious throne, you who have followed me will also sit on twelve thrones, judging the twelve tribes of Israel.

Wick is the Spirit

• Wicks burn down evenly with wax.

• every Candle is Choose with a wick with thin, braided wicks.

• there are those candles with very thick wicks and those with a wire core holding the wick upright.

• there are those who have multiple wick candles.

• Candle wicks are often made of chemically grown, cotton that has been bleached using dioxins.

• Wicks with metal down the middle are the most (hazardous), as they contain lead

1 Corinthians 6:19 "Do you not know that your bodies are temples of the Holy Spirit, who is in you, whom you have received from God? You are not your own;"

The Spirit of the LORD will rest on him-- the Spirit of wisdom and of understanding, the Spirit of counsel and of might, the Spirit of the knowledge and fear of the LORD— Isaiah 11:2

Matthew 3:16 As soon as Jesus was baptized, He went up out of the water. Suddenly the heavens were opened, and he saw the Spirit of God descending like a dove and resting on Him.

John 1:32 Then John testified, "I saw the Spirit descending from heaven like a dove and resting on Him.

John 16:13 However, when the Spirit of truth comes, He will guide you into all truth. For He will not speak on His own, but He will speak what He hears, and He will declare to you what is to come.

1 Corinthians 1:30 It is because of Him that you are in Christ Jesus, who has become for us wisdom from God: our righteousness, holiness, and redemption.

Ephesians 1:17 and asking that the God of our Lord Jesus Christ, the glorious Father, may give you a spirit of wisdom and revelation in your knowledge of Him.

Ephesians 1:18 I ask that the eyes of your heart may be enlightened, so that you may know the hope of His calling, the riches of His glorious inheritance in the saints,

Colossians 2:3 in whom are hidden all the treasures of wisdom and knowledge.

2 Timothy 1:7 For God has not given us a spirit of timidity, but of power, love, and self-control.

Revelation 1:4 John, To the seven churches in the province of Asia: Grace and peace to you from Him who is and was and is to come, and from the sevenfold Spirit before His throne,

Exodus 28:3 "You shall speak to all the skillful persons whom I have endowed with the spirit of wisdom, that they make Aaron's garments to consecrate him, that he may minister as priest to Me.

Romans 8:9 You, however, are not in the realm of the flesh but are in the realm of the Spirit, if indeed the Spirit of God lives in you. And if anyone does not have the Spirit of Christ, they do not belong to Christ.

Different candle size–different colors.

1 Corinthians 12:8 To one there is given through the Spirit a message of wisdom, to another a message of knowledge by means of the same Spirit,

Romans 15:14 I myself am convinced, my brothers, that you yourselves are full of goodness, brimming with knowledge, and able to instruct one another.

1 Corinthians 2:6 Among the mature, however, we speak a message of wisdom--but not the wisdom of this age or of the rulers of this age, who are coming to nothing.

1 Corinthians 2:11 For who among men knows the thoughts of man except his own spirit within him? So too, no one knows the thoughts of God except the Spirit of God.

1 Corinthians 2:16 "For who has known the mind of the Lord, so as to instruct Him?" But we have the mind of Christ.

1 Corinthians 14:6 Now, brothers, if I come to you speaking in tongues, how will I benefit you, unless I bring you some revelation or knowledge or prophecy or teaching?

1 Corinthians 14:26 What then shall we say, brothers? When you come together, everyone has a psalm or a teaching, a revelation, a tongue, or an interpretation. All of these must be done to build up the church.

2 Corinthians 1:12 And this is our boast: Our conscience testifies that we have conducted ourselves in the world, and especially in

relation to you, in the holiness and sincerity that are from God--not in worldly wisdom, but in the grace of God.

2 Corinthians 2:14 But thanks be to God, who always leads us triumphantly as captives in Christ and through us spreads everywhere the fragrance of the knowledge of Him.
2 Corinthians 4:6 For God, who said, "Let light shine out of darkness," made His light shine in our hearts to give us the light of the knowledge of the glory of God in the face of Jesus Christ.

2 Corinthians 6:6 in purity, knowledge, patience, and kindness; in the Holy Spirit and in sincere love;

The giftwrap and unwrap

Different candle – Perfect giftwrap – unwrap for glory. Glory mean's: spot of light celebrity, fame, renown, praise, honor.

Every good and perfect gift is from above, coming down from the Father of the heavenly lights, who does not change like shifting shadows. James 1:17

- 1 Corinthians 9:24 Do you not know that in a race all the runners run, but only one gets the prize? Run in such a way as to get the prize.
- Matthew 23:19 You blind men! Which is greater: the gift, or the altar that makes the gift sacred?
- Psalm 85:12 Indeed, the LORD will give what is good, And our land will yield its produce.

Psalm 102:27 "But You are the same, And Your years will not come to an end.

Psalm 136:7 To Him who made the great lights, For His lovingkindness is everlasting:

Daniel 2:22 "It is He who reveals the profound and hidden things; He knows what is in the darkness, And the light dwells with Him.

Malachi 3:6 "For I, the LORD, do not change; therefore you, O sons of Jacob, are not consumed.

Matthew 7:11So if you who are evil know how to give good gifts to your children, how much more will your Father in heaven give good things to those who ask Him!

John 3:3 Jesus replied, "Truly, truly, I tell you, no one can see the kingdom of God unless he is born again."

John 3:27 John replied, "A man can receive only what is given him from heaven.

1 Timothy 6:16 He alone is immortal and dwells in unapproachable light. No one has ever seen Him, nor can anyone see Him. To Him be honor and eternal dominion! Amen.

James 3:15
Such wisdom does not come from above, but is earthly, unspiritual, demonic.

Oil of Grace

- The oil is the grace –Romans 11:6 And if by grace, then it cannot be based on works; if it were, grace would no longer be grace.

Warning of the Use

1. Remove plastic wrapping before use (take away yourself before being used by God.)
2. All candle may drip or drain (swat, get weak)
3. do not burn for more than 4 hours per use (work with time not overtime)
4. Allow candle to cool before relighting (relax, take break before going back)
5. Avoid smoke (avoid people with trouble or problems)
6. For more service please call 1-800-God. Or 1-800-Have faith.

The word, the works and life

1. The word, (The word of fire, Spirit and Fire)
2. The works, (Let light shine out of darkness, He Opened their eyes)
3. The life. (Example, In him was life)

The word of fire

Acts 2:3 They saw what seemed to be tongues of fire that separated and came to rest on each of them.

Matthew 3:11 I baptize you with water for repentance. But after me comes one who is more powerful than I, whose sandals I am not worthy to carry. He will baptize you with the Holy Spirit and fire.

Acts 2:2 Suddenly a sound like the blowing of a violent wind came from heaven and filled the whole house where they were sitting.

Acts 2:4 All of them were filled with the Holy Spirit and began to speak in other tongues as the Spirit enabled them.

Spirit and Fire

- 1 John 4:4 You, dear children, are from God and have overcome them, because the one who is in you is greater than the one who is in the world.
- 2 Corinthians 5:17 therefore, if anyone is in Christ, the new creation has come: The old has gone, the new is here
- 1 John 4:2 This is how you can recognize the Spirit of God: Every spirit that acknowledges that Jesus Christ has come in the flesh is from God,

Let light shine out of darkness

- 2 Corinthians 4:6 For God, who said, "Let light shine out of darkness," made his light shine in our hearts to give us the light of the knowledge of God's glory displayed in the face of Christ.

- John 8:12 When Jesus spoke again to the people, he said, "I am the light of the world. Whoever follows me will never walk in darkness, but will have the light of life."
- Genesis 1:3 And God said, "Let there be light," and there was light.

- Ephesians 1:18 I pray that the eyes of your heart may be enlightened in order that you may know the hope to which he has called you, the riches of his glorious inheritance in his holy people,
  John 8:12

Their eyes

- Acts 26:18 to open their eyes and turn them from darkness to light, and from the power of Satan to God, so that they may receive forgiveness of sins and a place among those who are sanctified by faith in me.

- Joel 2:28 "And it shall come to pass afterward, that I will pour out my Spirit on all flesh; your sons and your daughters shall prophesy, your old men shall dream dreams, and your young men shall see visions.
- Acts 2:17 In the last days, God says, I will pour out my Spirit on all people. Your sons and daughters will prophesy, your young men will see visions, your old men will dream dreams.

Making an Example

- 1 Peter 2:21 To this you were called, because Christ suffered for you, leaving you an example, that you should follow in his steps.
- John 13:15 I have set you an example that you should do as I have done for you.
- Matthew 11:29 Take my yoke upon you and learn from me, for I am gentle and humble in heart, and you will find rest for your souls.

In him was /is life

- John 1:4 In him was life, and that life was the light of all mankind.
- John 9:5 While I am in the world, I am the light of the world.
- John 3:19This is the verdict: Light has come into the world, but people loved darkness instead of light because their deeds were evil.
- Matthew 5:14 "You are the light of the world. A town built on a hill cannot be hidden.

Apostolic coving For Light

I welcome you into your own year of LIGHT on every side in Jesus Mighty name.

1. Father, my exceeding greatness will not be undermined throughout this year and beyond, in Jesus Name. (Isaiah 54:3, Zechariah 1:18-21)

2. Father, let my head be lifted above all my enemies on every side, in Jesus Name. (Psalm 30:1)

3. Father, let my mouth be enlarged over all my mockers by making my life exceedingly great, in Jesus Name. (1 Samuel 2:1)

4. Father, let every step that I take, in this year, cause me to move forward, in Jesus Name. (Proverbs 4:18, 2 Corinthians 3:18)

5. Father, let every small project and effort that I undertake, in this year, lead me into abundant greatness, in Jesus Name. (Job 8:7)

6. Father, let all my long-term desires for change and greatness be granted in this year, in Jesus Name. (Job 6:8)

7. Father, let all the blessings that you gave me, in previous years, be added unto me. None of my past achievements shall fall apart, in this year, in Jesus Name. (Psalm 115:13-14)

8. Father, take away every stumbling block to my Agenda of Exceeding Greatness throughout 2017 and beyond, in Jesus Name. (Isaiah 57:14, Job 12:14, Revelations 3:7)

9. Father, let our Agenda of Exceeding Greatness for "Dominion Families" be personally and visibly confirmed in my own life and in all the things that I do in this year, in Jesus Name. (2 Kings 7:1-3, Mark 16:20)

10. Father, let me and my family members be spared and protected from all evil works, destructions and reproaches, in this year, in Jesus Name. (Psalm 91:1-16, Joel 2:17)

11. Father, let all the mouths of my enemies and the mockers of my faith, in Christ Jesus, be permanently shut by the reasons of your undeniable favor in 2017, in Jesus Name. (Psalm 86:13-17)

12. Father, let every device of the wicked, targeted against my life, be destroyed throughout the year, in Jesus Name. (Job 5:12-13, Isaiah 54:17

13. Father, cause my feet not to meet with wicked and unreasonable men and women and destiny destroyers throughout the year and beyond, in Jesus Name. (2 Thessalonians 3:2-3)

14. Father, as I obey your word, make me to be above all challenges and circumstances throughout the year, in Jesus Name. (Deuteronomy 28:1)

15. Father, let me enjoy unparalleled and accelerated increase in all my endeavors throughout year, in Jesus Name. (Deuteronomy 28:4)

16. Father, let your goodness and mercy accompany me throughout my journey in this year, in Jesus Name. (Psalm 23:6)

17. Father, add all the good things of life to me daily throughout the year. I shall not lack any good thing as I serve and seek you, in Jesus Name. (Psalm 34:10, Exodus 23:25-26, Mathew 6:33)

18. Father, let me enjoy your divine presence from the beginning of the year until the end, culminating in "my unlimited progress", "my unspeakable joy" and "my uninterrupted peace", in Jesus Name. (Deuteronomy 11:12)

19. Father, by the blood of Jesus, let my life and my entire household be preserved and exempted from all trouble and troublemakers in the year, in Jesus Name. (Galatians 6:17)

20. Father, let all people acknowledge the undeniable aura of your blessings upon my life, throughout the year and beyond, in Jesus Name. (Isaiah 61:9)

21. Father, let there be no single occurrence of loss of life, property or material blessings in my family. Let only the voices of joy,

gladness and thanksgiving become a daily routine throughout the year, in Jesus Name. (Isaiah 51:3, Numbers 31:49)

22. Father, I cover myself and my entire family with the blood of Jesus against the arrows of the devil and his agents throughout the year, in Jesus Name. (Zechariah 9:11)

23. Father, let my mouth be filled with laughter and my tongue with singing throughout the year, in Jesus Name. (Psalm 126:2)

24. Father, let me enjoy angelic protection in all my journeys, "going out and coming in," throughout the year, in Jesus Name. (Psalm 91:11)

Prophetic Release for Light.

This year of light, bring out the bright futures of God children. More over this year will pushing us to step into change to receive new blessings from the father. It is a year of new sites to step in too, new work to beginning, new connections with people and entering in to saving lives and wining souls for Jesus.

We are to always be in prayer to know and recognizing the times and seasons we are in is acknowledging the prophetic power of the season and what that means for your life. When you actively align yourself with what God is doing in this time, you will see breakthrough! As an Apostle, I want to make five prophetic declarations of blessing over you to stir your faith and activate transformation in your life.

As you read these decrees, say them out loud and continue declaring them over yourself for the days and weeks to come. Words are extremely powerful!

Proverbs 18:21 says "The tongue has the power of life and death.."

You have the choice to either bless or curse yourself with your words. Choose to bless yourself and be expectant for transformation to come.

1. THE POWER OF THE HOLY SPIRIT

I decree a blessing over you that you will be full of the power of the Holy Spirit, be activated in the gifts of the Spirit and shift the spiritual atmosphere by His holy presence wherever you go.

In Acts 1:8, before Jesus ascends back into heaven, He says:

"But you shall receive power when the Holy Spirit has come upon you; and you shall be witnesses to Me in Jerusalem, and in all Judea and Samaria, and to the end of the earth".

If you are a born-again believer, you have the Holy Spirit but do you know His power? When we have an encounter with His power, we are launched into a more fruitful and victorious walk with Jesus.

For many men and women of God, there is a distinct experience of infilling of the Holy Spirit during which they receive His power. I had such an experience in 2004 in a small

congregation In Minnesota USA (Cottage Grove.) During a time of worship, I began to weep, encountering His deep love and presence. I was then filled with an electrifying sensation throughout my body.

As this continued, I began to sob tears of joy. I knew that at that moment, God was anointing me for a purpose and empowering me for service.

This kind of encounter with the Holy Spirit can look different for everyone, but regardless of how it manifests, it is certainly a promise for all those who believe in Jesus Christ. Declare that you will be full of the Holy Spirit, and you will be filled with His power and His presence to see transformation take place in your life and in the lives of others.

2   GOD'S KINGDOM

I decree a blessing over you that you will seek first His Kingdom and His righteousness and will preach the Gospel of the Kingdom with signs and wonders following.

In Matthew 6, Jesus instructs us how to pray to our heavenly Father. A crucial part of that prayer is:

"Thy kingdom come, Thy will be done in earth, as it is in heaven."

The Kingdom of God connotes the rule and reign of God and the realm of His glorious presence, with all the healing, manifestations and miracles that come with it. Our role as the Body of Christ is to see that Kingdom advance on earth: in our homes, our workplaces, in the church, in schools and in public spaces. He wants to manifest His glory everywhere!

It is my heart to see the Body of Christ raised up as culture reformers. As you seek first His kingdom (Matthew 6:33) you will see His kingdom come to your own sphere of influence, bringing holy, righteous change. Remember- were saved to go to heaven *and* to bring heaven to earth!

3. FAMILY

I decree a blessing over all your relationships, beginning with your family: that God would bless your marriage and the fruit of your womb; that He would bless your children, your grandchildren and your friendships in His Church and in the marketplace; and that your entire family would be saved.

For those of you who are contending for your family to be saved, be encouraged by the fact that God brings not just individuals to Christ, but entire households. In Acts 16,

Paul and Silas are literally released from prison in a great miracle of God. Moved by the miracle he witnesses, the jailer asks them how he can be saved.

"They replied, "Believe in the Lord Jesus, and you will be saved— you and your household." Then they spoke the word of the Lord to him and to all the others in his house. At that hour of the night the jailer took them and washed their wounds; then immediately he and all his household were baptized. The jailer brought them into his house and set a meal before them; he was filled with joy because he had come to believe in God—he and his whole household." (Acts 16: 31-34)

I can testify that through coming into alignment with the promises of God, Sue and I have witnessed an entire generation of our family members come to Christ—what a blessing! Decree salvation over your family daily. It will stir your faith and you will see His promises come to pass!

4. PROSPERITY

I decree a blessing over your finances, that God will break the spirit of poverty off of you and your bloodline and that you will prosper financially; that God would bless you with the power to gain wealth; and that you would advance His Kingdom with your generosity.

The spirit of poverty keeps many in the Body of Christ mired in financial difficulty and debt. But God wants to prosper both our souls and our finances. Deuteronomy 28:11 says:

"The LORD will grant you abundant prosperity–in the fruit of your womb, the young of your livestock and the crops of your ground–in the land he swore to your ancestors to give you." (emphasis added)

God wants to empower us to build businesses, creatively gain wealth and grow so that we can bless others. If you give generously to others, you will be blessed. If you are contending for financial provision and growth, decree over yourself that God would bring you breakthrough and grow your ability to prosper financially. Imagine what great wealth could look like in the hands of Spirit-filled believers in Christ and how they could use it to advance the Kingdom of God.

5. DESTINY

I decree a blessing over you to be led by His Spirit and His Word, that you will know and obey His will and that you will fulfill your prophetic destiny.

Year of Light is a season to look forward and consider where we are headed and how we are fulfilling the great and wonderful plans that our heavenly Father has for us. Jeremiah 29:11 says:

"For I know the plans I have for you," declares the Lord, "plans to prosper you and not to harm you, plans to give you hope and a future."

We need the Word and the Holy Spirit to fulfill our destiny. When you meditate on and declare the Word of God, and when you are filled with the Holy Spirit, you will begin to experience the fulfillment of the wonderful purpose that God has for your life.

GO DEEPER

I encourage you to build up yourself and those around you with decrees of blessing, especially as we enter into this new season of promises fulfilled. Here are some resources to equip you on your walk of faith: As you consider your destiny and the transformative power God wants to impart to you, be inspired by testimonies of great men and women of God in The Reformer's Pledge.

- Read God Wants to Bless You! for more powerful decrees that bring about transformation and blessing.

I declare and decree that this is a year in which God has heard our cries for mercy and things are turning around.
"I love the LORD, for he heard my voice; he heard my cry for mercy. Because he turned his ear to me, I will call on him as long as I live." Psalm 116:1–2 NIV

2. I speak the opening of heavenly gates and ancient doors that will bring us into deeper relationship with You, God.
"Lift up your heads, you gates; be lifted up, you ancient doors, that the King of glory may come in." Psalm 24:7 NIV

3. We decree a time of renewing our strength and soaring in Your presence God.
"… but those who hope in the LORD will renew their strength. They will soar on wings like eagles; they will run and not grow weary, they will walk and not be faint." Isaiah 40:31 NIV

4. We declare that the times of spiritual hopelessness and disappointments have come to an end. This is a year of sudden good breaks.

"Unrelenting disappointment leaves you heartsick, but a sudden good break can turn life around." Proverbs 13:12 MSG

5. Make us ministers of reconciliation to offset injustices and bring healing to people everywhere we go.
"All this is from God, who reconciled us to himself through Christ and gave us the ministry of reconciliation." 2 Corinthians 5:18 NIV

6. We agree with the new things that will bring spiritual refreshing to those who have been in the wilderness.
"Forget the former things; do not dwell on the past. See, I am doing a new thing! Now it springs up; do you not perceive it? I am making a way in the wilderness and streams in the wasteland." Isaiah 43:18–19 NIV

7. We declare a new day, as God's light shines on and through us.
"Arise, shine, for your light has come, and the glory of the LORD rises upon you." Isaiah 60:1 NIV

8. Help us to be stretched in order to receive all that you have for us.
"Enlarge the place of your tent, stretch your tent curtains wide, do not hold back; lengthen your cords, strengthen your stakes." Isaiah 54:2 NIV

9. Teach us to love, as You love us, God.
Jesus replied: "'Love the Lord your God with all your heart and with all your your God with all your heart and with all your soul and with all your mind.' This is the first and greatest

commandment. And the second is like it: 'Love your neighbor as yourself.' All the Law and the Prophets hang on these two commandments." Matthew 22:37–40 NIV

10. Give us wisdom to help those who need the love of God.
"And he will go on before the Lord, in the spirit and power of Elijah, to turn the hearts of the parents to their children and the disobedient to the wisdom of the righteous—to make ready a people prepared for the Lord." Luke 1:17 NIV

11. Grant us the ability to forgive and not judge others.
"Do not judge, and you will not be judged. Do not condemn, and you

will not be condemned. Forgive, and you will be forgiven. Give, and it will be given to you.

A good measure, pressed down, shaken together and running over, will be poured into your lap. For with the measure you use, it will be measured to you." Luke 6:37–38 NIV

12. We gladly receive any pruning needed in our lives in order for us to remain in You, Lord.
"I am the vine; you are the branches. If you remain in me and I in you, you will bear much fruit; apart from me you can do nothing. If you do not remain in me, you are like a branch that is thrown away and withers; such branches are picked up, thrown into the fire and burned." John 15:5–6 NIV

13. We decree that we will step into a place this year to have greater authority to see answers to the things we ask for in prayer.
"If you remain in me and my words remain in you, ask whatever you wish, and it will be done for you." John 15:7 NIV

14. We are in agreement with God's promises to pour out His Spirit on our descendants and declare that we will see them grow fast and strong.
"For I will pour water on the thirsty land, and streams on the dry ground; I will pour out my Spirit on your offspring, and my blessing on your descendants. They will spring up like grass in a meadow, like poplar trees by flowing streams. Some will say, 'I belong to the LORD; others will call themselves by the name of Jacob; still; others will call themselves by the name of Jacob; still others will write on their hand, 'The LORD's,' and will take the name Israel." Isaiah 44:3–5 NIV

15. Open opportunities for us to see who needs that deeper touch. Use us to bring healing to people who have been wounded and rejected.

"Go out quickly into the streets and alleys of the town and bring in the poor, the crippled, the blind and the lame." Luke 14:21b NI

16. We pray for the new sound from Heaven to be released on the Earth.
"And I heard a sound from heaven like the roar of rushing waters and like a loud peal of thunder. The sound I heard was like that of harpists playing their harps." Revelation 14:2 NIV

17. We declare and decree that we will live our lives this year above all the negativity around us. We look for doors of opportunity and ask for eyes to see all that you are doing God.

"After this I looked, and there before me was a door standing open in heaven. And the voice I had first heard speaking to me like a trumpet said, 'Come up here, and I will show you what must take place after this.'" Revelation 4:1 NIV

We are salt of the earth and light of the world. We are because that is what God has made us, and that is what Christ has declared us to be. Not for our sake, but for the sake of the world, that through us the world might see, and give glory to God. Let us go from this place, empowered by God to be what we are: salt of the earth, light of the world.

THE BEGINNING OF ALL BLESSING

God is intentional in blessing you—He wants you to bear fruit for the sake of others. The foundation of all blessing is the cross.

In the death and resurrection of Jesus Christ, we exchange our problems, sickness and difficulty for His glorious salvation and blessings.

His blessings are not earned—they are rooted in God's great love for us and His infinite mercy. We have been delivered from curses through the cross.

As you decree transformation in your life during this season, meditate on the fact that Jesus Christ paid it all for you to be saved from eternal death and to live abundantly in this life.

The End...

Yet is a New Beginning. Arise and Shine for your Light Has come.
Isaiah 60:1

What have you Learned in all three Columns? Write three or more things that you may implements in your personal life?

1)

2)

3)

Books by the Author

Sheka Mansaray

1. The Tears of My Father: My Gift to the World

2. DESERT ROSE: WORDS FOR THOUGHTS

3. Warfare Time: Spiritual Warfare

4. Carrier of Christ's Light: Arise, shine, for your light has come

Author Biography

Sheka Mansaray is the founder and Pastor of "Faith Embassy International Ministries" a multi-cultural, non-denominational church. Mansaray is the founder of Sheka Mansaray Ministries, a partnership-based outreach ministry with a solid Apostolic and Prophetic Mandate. Mansaray is also the founder of "Alpha Business Network" a network of current and future business owners. He is a gifted Poet, Writer, Philanthropist, Entrepreneur, and Author. Sheka Mansaray is a husband, happily married to his wife, Nanah Mansaray; and a father to their two children, daughter, Faith Mansaray; and Son, Sheka Jeremiah Mansaray Jr.

www.ingramcontent.com/pod-product-compliance
Lightning Source LLC
Chambersburg PA
CBHW062046090426
42740CB00016B/3040